Ri

Rise And

Be Healed

Dr. Eldon & Wanell Bollinger

With Contributions by Dr. Harold Bollinger

www.amazon.com — Title ID: 6336742

ISBN-13: 978-1534617469

ISBN-10: 1534617469

Contact us; it's easy! See *Contact Us*, page 190—Thank You!

Most Bible Scriptures quoted within this publication are from the *King James Version* (KJV) Bible unless otherwise indicated. Quoted non-KJV Bible Scriptures will include its abbreviated Bible version (in parentheses) from which they are cited from, e.g., Amplified Bible (AMP), New King James Version (NKJV), New International Version (NIV), Weymouth New Testament (WNT), and many others.

All Bible Scriptures are presented as originally written and verbatim, however, the author added *[bracketed italic]* modern English words to aid the reader to what the author believes the Scriptures are conveying *[communicating]*, e.g., Mark 16:17, "…in my name shall they *[you]* cast out demons; they *[we]* shall speak with new tongues.", or in John 6:47 (KJV) Jesus says, "Verily, verily *[truly* or *honestly]*, I say unto you, He that believeth on *[in]* me hath everlasting *[eternal]* life."

Because of the dynamic nature of the World-Wide-Web (Internet), any URL addresses, Web-links, email addresses/links or other Internet listings within this publication may have changed since its release and may no longer be valid.

Table of Contents

Table of Contents

Blank page added for 'Notes.'

CHAPTER 1

HEALING BELONGS TO YOU TODAY

It's God's Will for all of his children to be healed.

Jesus healed all who came to Him.

Jesus is the same yesterday, today, and forever.

Jesus Himself took our infirmities (diseases) and bore (carried) our sicknesses.

"If ye ask any thing in my name, I will do it."—John 14:14 (KJV).

"What so ever you desire, when you pray believe that you receive it, and you shall have it."—Mark 11:24 (KJV).

Great multitudes followed Jesus, and he healed them all. "And whatsoever ye shall ask in my name, that will I do...."—John 14:13 (KJV).

Jesus and His Word are the Healers

Jesus Christ went about healing the sick, and He has never changed: "Jesus Christ the same yesterday, today, and forever."—Hebrews 13:8 (NKJV).

"And Jesus went about all the cities and villages, teaching in their synagogues, and preaching the gospel of the kingdom, and healing every sickness and every disease among the people."—Matthew 9:35 (KJV).

"And whithersoever he entered, into villages, or cities, or country, they laid the sick in the streets, and besought *[begged]* him that they might touch if it were but the border of his garment: and as many as touched him were made whole."—Mark 6:56 (KJV).

"How God anointed Jesus of Nazareth with the Holy Ghost and with power: who went about doing good and healing all that were oppressed of the devil; for God was with him."—Acts 10:38 (KJV).

"And when he had called unto him his twelve disciples, he gave them power against unclean spirits, to cast them out, and to heal all manner of sickness and all manner of disease."—Matthew 10:1 (KJV).

Our Commission Today

God answered and said, my son just as I was with Jesus, so will I be with you. You go and cast out devils. You cleanse the lepers. You raise the dead. I give you power over all the power of the enemy. Do not be afraid. Be strong. Be courageous. I am with you as I was with Jesus. No demons shall be able to stand before you all the days of your life. I used men and women then, but now I desire to use you.

Rise and Be Healed in Jesus Name;
It is God's Will for All of His Children.

Today is our day, we need to roll up our sleeves and go do the works that Jesus did when He was here, and God wants us to face the world and to meet the needs of the people today just as Peter did when he was here. He tells us to open the blind eyes, unstopped the deaf ears, and break the bands of Satan and his sicknesses. The world is depending on us to do that. We have this power within us. It is given to us by God, and we must act on it today. We must begin today to work in Jesus name, in His stead, and as He instructed.

You are to heal the sick, cast out evil spirits, set the captive free, raise the dead, and do the things that Jesus did when He was here on the earth. Peter, James, John, Elijah, Paul, and all of the others were just ordinary people like you and me. They yielded their lives to God, believed His Word, and acted on it. This is what we can do, and as we do, we will see the same results that they did. The world is depending on us.

God wants to use you too. If you will obey his voice and act on it, all things are possible to you.

Luke 1:37 (KJV) says, "For with God nothing shall be impossible." Now add the promise of Matthew 17:20 (KJV); "…nothing shall be impossible unto you."

God is looking for people who will obey his voice. When God called Moses, He needed an obedient person

who He could use. When He called Joshua, David, Rahab, Esther, and many others, He needed someone obedient to His call. When Peter was anointed at Pentecost, God needed an obedient vessel. People have always used methods, but God employs people. God is still looking for people that will be obedient to his call.

God needs people today. He chooses ordinary people like you and me. Be God's instrument for today. Who knows whether you come to the kingdom for such a time as this?

God wants us to face our world and to meet her needs today as Peter did in his day. This is our day of ministry.

If you are a born-again Christian, you can do everything God or his son Jesus said that you could do. Jesus said, "...They shall lay hands on the sick, and they shall recover."—Mark 16:18 (KJV). That is what will happen when you lay hands on the sick expecting God to keep his word.

Jesus meant what He said. If the Word of God means anything, it means what it says. God will do what He said He would do, and we can do what God says we can do.

You will never grow spiritually by negative confession or by confessing what you cannot do. Learn to make your admission big and declare what you can

do according to what God said in His Word, and you will begin to grow spiritually.

Paul says: "I can do all things through Christ which strengthen this me."—Philippians 4:13 (KJV).

Paul never spoke of what he could not do, but of what he could do. Believe that you can do everything God says you can do. Believe that you are what God says you are. We are more than conquerors through Him that loved us, we are victors. We are over-comers; make your confession big and bold.

'Notes'

Blank page added for 'Notes.' ⇨⇨⇨

CHAPTER 2

SICKNESS IS FROM SATAN

We must begin to understand that God wants you to be well and that Satan wants you to be sick and suffering. You need to understand clearly, that sicknesses are from Satan, and not from God: that Satan has put them on us, and not God. Illness and disease are from the devil, and his job is to steal, to kill, and to destroy.

Blindness is caused by the devil. Mark 9:25 (KJV); "When Jesus saw that the people came running together, he rebuked the foul spirit, saying unto him, Thou dumb and deaf spirit, I charge thee, come out of him, and enter no more into him."

Luke 13:11-13 (KJV); "[11-]And, behold, there was a woman which had a spirit of infirmity eighteen years, and was bowed together, and could in no wise lift up herself. [12-]And when Jesus saw her, he called her to him, and said unto her, Woman, thou art loosed from thine infirmity. [13-]And he laid his hands on her: and immediately she was made straight, and glorified God."

Luke 13:6 (KJV); "And ought not this woman, being a daughter of Abraham, whom Satan hath bound, lo,

~ 7 ~

these eighteen years, be loosed from this bond on the sabbath day?"

We must remember that Jesus went about healing all that were oppressed of the devil. The Scripture in Acts 10:38 (KJV) clearly says that all sick people whom Jesus healed had been "…oppressed of the devil." In those days, sicknesses were identified as Satan's diseases; they do not belong to God's Children.

Luke 4:40-41 (KJV); "[40-]Now when the sun was setting, all they that had any sick with divers [various] diseases brought them unto him; and he laid hands on every one of them, and healed them. [41-]And devils also came out of many, crying out, and saying, you art Christ the son of God…."

Mark 1:22-25 (KJV); "[22-]…and Jesus taught them as one that had authority, and not as the scribes. [23-]And there was in their synagogue a man with an unclean spirit, and he cried out, [24-]Saying, let us alone; what have we to do with thee, thou Jesus of Nazareth? Are you come to destroy us? I know thee who art, the holy one of God. [25-]And Jesus rebuked him, saying, hold your peace, and come out of him."

These signs shall follow them that believe, "In my name, they shall cast out devils."—Mark 16:17. Mary Magdalene was possessed of seven devils, yet one man, anointed of God, cast out all seven devils. It proves that all of our natural strength and wisdom is helpless before the devil, yet all the devils in hell are weak before one

believer who is anointed of God. It also proves that demons recognize and obey those who have power over them. All born-again Christians that act of faith have that power and authority.

Isaiah 54:17 (KJV); "No weapon that is formed against thee *[you]* shall prosper; and every tongue that rise against thee *[you]* in judgment thou *[you]* shall condemn. This is the heritage *[birthright]* of the servants of the LORD, and their righteousness is of *[from]* me, says the LORD."

The Sickness Problem

There is NO sickness problem. There is merely a problem of the believers coming to know his inheritance in Christ.

1 Peter 2:24 (KJV); "Who his own self bare our sins in his body on the tree, that we, dead to sins, should live unto righteousness: by whose stripes ye were healed."

God wants us to know that when He laid our sins and sicknesses on Jesus and Jesus bore them away; it was to the end in that sin and disease should no longer have dominion over us.

He also wants us to know that sickness and disease do not belong to the family of God.

If there should be any sickness among us, it is because of a lack of the knowledge of our rights and

privileges in our redemption. It is due to a lack of understanding of the fact that God has settled the disease problem in redemption.

We should be as free from the fear of sickness as we are free from the condemnation of sin. Both are of Satan. Our Heavenly Father can see no sickness in the new creation (man). He put it all on, Christ.

When we recognize the fact that our sickness was laid on Christ, and that He bore our disease in his body on the tree, and that by his stripes we are healed, it will be the end of the dominion of disease and illness in our lives.

But this knowledge is of no value until your heart says, 'Surely He has borne my diseases and my pains, and by His stripes, I am healed,' just as though you were the only sick person in the world. Jesus was made sin with our sin, and He was made ill with our diseases.

In the mind of our Heavenly Father, we are perfectly healed and free from sin because God laid our diseases and our sin upon the Lord Jesus Christ.

Sickness is judging you falsely for it is your birthright to live in health. You condemn it with the Word of God and command it to leave your body.

Psalm 102:19-20 (KJV); "[19-]For He hath looked down from the height of his sanctuary; from heaven did the Lord behold the earth; [20-]To hear the sighing and

groaning of the prisoner; to loose *[release]* those who are appointed to death."

If you are born-again, then YOU are not appointed to death but unto life in Christ Jesus. The Word tells us that He *[God]* who the son sets free is free indeed! Take hold of and insist upon your covenant right of freedom today in Jesus' Name. Command the devil, sickness, disease, pain, and suffering to GO in Jesus' Name. You have another appointment with Him, and that appointment is supernatural, overflowing, and abundant life in Jesus Christ our Lord. You may feel like a prisoner because of your circumstance, but rejoice because God's Will is to <u>*RELEASE*</u> you from it. Begin to praise Him for it.

Let's look at 1 John 3:8 (KJV); "…For this purpose, the Son of God was manifested *[demonstrated]*, that he might destroy the works of the devil." Now look at Colossians 2:15 (KJV); "And having spoiled principalities and powers, he made a show of them openly, triumphing of the over them in it."

According to the Scriptures, Jesus has destroyed the works of the devil, spoiled his power, and triumphant it over him. Since Satan's work has been destroyed, his power has been ruined; he must be a defeated foe.

Jesus' trial was our trial. His victory was our victory. He did nothing for Himself, but for all of us. He defeated Satan for us. He spoiled his power for us. He destroyed his work for us. He conquered him for us.

Can you afford to subject yourself to Satan's domain any longer? Never. Arise from his bondage. Confess that you are the conqueror. Then be sure to hold fast your confession of faith without wavering for He is faithful that promised! Maintain your confession of God's Word. Every believer can become a devil master overnight. When Jesus arose from the dead, He left an eternally defeated Satan behind Him. Always think of Satan as an eternally defeated foe. Think of Satan as one whom Jesus, and you in Jesus name, have entire dominion and authority over.

The Bible declares; "For we are his workmanship, created in Christ Jesus…."—Ephesians 2:10 (KJV). If any person is in Christ, that person is a new creation. We are positively made 'new' in Christ.

'Notes'

⇦⇦⇦   Blank page added for 'Notes.'

Blank page added for 'Notes.'

CHAPTER 3

YOU CAN BE HEALED

Written by Dr. Harold Bollinger

"…By whose *[Jesus']* stripes I am healed."—1 Peter 2:24 (KJV).

It is God's Will that you prosper and be in health, just as my soul prospers (see 3 John 2).

The Lord is my healer (Exodus 15:26).

Jesus came that I may enjoy life and have it in overflowing abundance (John 10:10).

As I serve the Lord, sickness is taken from my midst (Exodus 23:25).

Healing is one of God's benefits (Psalm 103:3).

Jesus is the serpent on the pole lifted up in the New Covenant for my healing and deliverance (John 3:14).

God sent His Word and healed me (Psalm 107:20).

I pay attention to God's Word, for it is life to my body and health to my flesh (Proverbs 4:20-22).

God gives me good and perfect gifts. He has no sickness or disease to give me (James 1:17).

As I submit to God and resist the devil, he must flee from me. Sickness and disease must also flee from me (James 4:7).

Jesus is able and willing to heal me (Matthew 8:1-2).

Jesus can heal me through my believing, receiving, and speaking His Word or through the touch of another believer who is empowered by the Holy Ghost (Mark 16:18).

Jesus paid for all sin and sickness at Calvary (Matthew 8:17).

Jesus is the same yesterday, today, and forever (Hebrews 13:8).

Because the Lord is my refuge and habitation, no evil or plague shall come nigh my dwelling (Psalm 91:9-11).

I am redeemed with the blood of Jesus Christ (1 Peter 1:19).

I am justified by faith, not by works of the law (Galatians 3:13).

Jesus redeemed me from the curse of the law (Galatians 3:13).

~ 16 ~

The blessings of Abraham have come upon me (Deuteronomy 28:1-14).

Jesus legally redeemed me from the bondage of sickness and disease and every other work of the enemy (Luke 13:10-17).

Jesus bore my griefs *[sicknesses]* and carried my sorrows *[pains]* (Isaiah 53:4).

Jesus was wounded, bruised, and beaten for my sins, sicknesses, and diseases (Isaiah 53:5).

I discern the Lord's body and receive all that He has provided for me, including healing for my physical body (1 Corinthians11:23-30).

I am diligent to pray for my brothers and sisters in Christ that they may become all God has called them to be (1 Corinthians 11:23-30).

To touch Jesus is to be made whole. I touched Jesus today through prayer and faith (Mark 5:25-34).

The resurrection power of Jesus Christ flows from my tongue as I speak words of life (Proverbs 18:21).

I have been given authority in the name of Jesus to speak to the mountains that I face. As I command the mountains of sickness, despair, hopelessness, and lack to be removed in Jesus' name, they must go and be

replaced with the fullness of God's blessings (Mark 11:22-23).

Because I meditate on the Word of God day and night, God's prosperity and success are overtaking me in all realms of life (Joshua 1:8).

The measure of faith God gave me is growing by leaps and bounds (Romans 12:3).

Because my faith is growing, nothing is impossible unto me (Matthew 17:20).

Jesus is moved with compassion on my behalf. He wants me healed because of His great love for me (Matthew 14:14).

Satan cannot dominate or oppress my life because Jesus came to set me free (1 John 3:8; Acts 10:38).

Just as God's Grace was sufficient to cause Paul to overcome all of Satan's buffeting, God's Grace causes me to defeat Satan's buffetings (2 Corinthians 12:7).

Christ Jesus causes me to triumph in every area of life (2 Corinthians 12:9-10).

I will rise above anything and everything the devil throws at me. Nothing can keep me down for I am more than a conqueror in Christ Jesus (Romans 8:35-39).

Today I will rise to new life from the depression and prostration in which circumstances have kept me (Isaiah 60:1).

Jesus is the author of abundant life, while it is Satan who steals kills and destroys (John 10:10).

The days of my life are seventy years; and if by reason of strength eighty (Psalm 90:10).

Long life is mine because I obey and honor my parents in the Lord (Ephesians 6:1-3, Exodus 20:12).

My obedience to the Lord prolongs my life (Proverbs 10:27).

By Using What the Bible
Promises, Believers Can Receive Healing

One promise comes from 1 Peter 2:24, "…By whose *[Jesus']* stripes, you were healed." This is a simple and irrefutable promise. Jesus suffered when He was beaten. We all remember that piece of Scripture. We also must remember as a believer we are healed by that beating and by the stripes He received.

3 John 2 brings another promise to us. It says it is God's Will that I prosper and be in health just as my soul prospers. If God helps a believer to flourish, He will also help the believer to receive health until it is the believer's time to return to the Lord. Our soul prospers

by praying, reading the Word of God and doing His Will. Then our soul will be well and so will our body.

'The Lord is my healer' is written in Exodus 15:26. Who else but the Lord could heal the believer? Only the Lord guides and directs us toward our healing whether it is in the soul or in the body. God created us, and we must follow his orders because He created us for a specific purpose. He established His believers to help unbelievers to believe and to become healthy in soul and body.

John says in John 10:10, "Jesus came that I might enjoy life and have it in overflowing abundance." Abundance does not mean in illness or despair, but with God as our guide, we can live a healthy life in happiness and peace in our soul knowing He is guiding our every move.

In Exodus 23:25 it is written, "As I serve the Lord, sickness is taken from my midst." Isn't that a beautiful feeling? We can serve the Lord and be healed and show others if they believe, they can also be healed.

Any believer should know healing is one of God's benefits. Psalm 103:3 says this is true. There are many benefits to living under God's broad umbrella. He has enough love to help everyone in the whole world if they just come to Him. He can heal everyone who believes if they only go to Him. If one can't kneel, sit and pray that you will be able to follow the Lord. He will heal body and soul. But belief must come first.

Jesus is like the serpent on the pole lifted up in the New Covenant for my healing and deliverance, according to John 3:14. Do you read the Bible? The serpent was put on a pole for the Israelites to be healed of the serpent's bite. This serpent can also be known as the devil. We can be healed of the devil's bite by putting God in front of us to take care of us as a believer. The devil can cause all kinds of illnesses of both the body and the soul. Remember God loves you and wants to see a believer as a healthy person so they can make others healthy.

"God sent His Word and healed me." This quote is found in Psalm 107:20. Who was the Word? The Word was Jesus. This brings us back to the beginning. God was the Word, and the Word was with God (John 1:1). Jesus has been with the Father from the time God created the world. He sent His Word and His Word healed me, lowly me, a believer but just a little part of the world. Jesus was the Word He sent to heal me. Praise the Lord!

According to Proverbs 4:20, "I pay attention to God's Word for it is life to my body and health to my flesh." Isn't that an incredible statement? If we as a believer pay attention to God's Word, then we will have a good life in our body and health for our flesh.

A perfect ending for this chapter on Bible promises given to us to receive healing comes from James 1:17; 'God gives me good and perfect gifts. He has no sickness or disease to give me.' If you are a believer,

please believe this statement. If you are not yet a believer, learn God loves you, yes you! All we need to remember is John 3:16. Read it and accept Jesus as your Saviour and go with Him wherever He leads. He will keep you healthy, body and soul.

'Notes'

⇐⇐⇐   Blank page added for 'Notes.'

Blank page added for 'Notes.'

CHAPTER 4

PHYSICAL HEALING

Isaiah 53:4-5 (KJV); "⁴Surely He hath borne our griefs *[sicknesses]*, and carried our sorrows *[pains]*: yet we did esteem Him stricken, smitten of God, and afflicted. ⁵But he was wounded for our transgressions, he was bruised for our iniquities: the chastisement of our peace was upon him; and by His stripes we are healed."

The last part of this verse, '...by His stripes, we are healed' is not talking about spiritual healing, as some have taught, but definite physical healing. God does not "heal" a human spirit; He recreates it. He does, however, heal our bodies and minds. This clearly shows that your healing was paid for at the cross!

How could an Old Testament person understand the idea of Christ dying for our sins (our transgressions and iniquities)—actually bearing the punishment that we deserved? The sacrifices suggested this idea, but it is one thing to kill a lamb, and something entirely different to think of God's chosen servant as that Lamb. But God was pulling aside the curtain of time to let the people of Isaiah's day look ahead to the suffering of the future Messiah and the resulting forgiveness made available to all mankind.

Jeremiah 33:6 (KJV); "Behold, I will bring it *[you]* health and cure, and I will cure them *[you]*, and will reveal unto them *[you]* the abundance of peace and truth."

God is ready to answer our prayers, but we must ask for his assistance. Surely God could take care of our needs without our asking. But when we ask Him, we are acknowledging that He alone is God and that we cannot accomplish in our own strength all that is his domain to do. When we ask, we must humble ourselves, lay aside our willfulness and worry, and determine to obey Him.

Matthew 18:19 (KJV); "Again I say to you, that if two of you agree on Earth touching *[concerning]* anything that they shall ask, it shall be done for them of *[by]* my Father which is in heaven."

Jeremiah 30:17 (KJV); "For I will restore health unto thee *[you]*, and I will heal thee *[you]* of your wounds, saith the Lord...."

The medical language here conveys the idea that sin is terminal. Sinful people cannot be cured by being good, or being religious. Beware of putting your confidence in useless cures while your sin spreads and causes you pain. God alone can cure the disease of sin, but you must be willing to let Him do it.

The prayer of agreement is powerful–have someone agree with you for your healing!

Jesus looked ahead to a new day when He would be present with his followers not in body, but through his Holy Spirit. In the body of believers (the Church), the sincere agreement of two people is more powerful than the superficial agreement of thousands, because Christ's Holy Spirit is with them. Two or more believers, filled with the Holy Spirit, will pray according to God's Will; not their own, thus their requests will be granted.

Mark 11:24 (KJV); "Therefore I say to you, what things soever ye *[you]* desire *[ask]*, when you pray, believe that ye *[you]* receive them, and you will have them." Surely this includes healing!

Jesus, our example for prayer, prayed; "Everything is possible for you. "…Nevertheless, not what I Will, but what you *will*."—Mark 14:36 (NKJV). Our prayers are often motivated by our own interests and desires. We like to hear that we can have anything. But Jesus prayed with God's interests in mind. When we pray, we should express our desires, but want His Will above ours. Check yourself to see if your prayers focus on your interests or God's.

Isaiah 58:8 (AMPC); "Then shall your light break forth like the morning, and thy healing *[health]* shall spring forth speedily; your righteousness shall go before you, the glory of the Lord shall be thy rear guard."

We cannot be saved by deeds of service without faith in Christ, but our faith lacks sincerity if it doesn't reach out to others.

Psalm 41:3 (AMPC); "The Lord will sustain, refresh, *and* strengthen him on his bed of languishing; all his bed You [O Lord] will turn, change, *and* transform in his illness."

The Amplified Bible brings out the fullness of meaning in the original language. The phrase 'all his bed' in the Hebrew language has the meaning of; 'all that he is afflicted with, or all of his conditions that he is lying with.' It is always His Will to turn, change and transform our mourning into dancing (see Psalm 30:11).

1 Thessalonians 5:23 (KJV); "And the very God of peace sanctify you wholly; and I pray God your whole spirit and soul and body be preserved blameless *[sound, complete and intact]* unto the coming of our Lord Jesus Christ."

It is evident in this passage that wholeness, wellness, and health, are for the complete make-up of man, spiritual, mental, and physical.

The spirit, soul, and body refer not so much to the distinct parts of a person as to the entire being of a person. This expression is Paul's way of saying that God must be involved in every aspect of our lives. It is wrong to think that we can separate our spiritual lives from everything else, obeying God only in some ethereal sense or living for Him only one day each week. Christ must control all of us, not just a "religious" part.

1 Peter 2:24 (KJV); "Who his own self *[Himself]* bare our sins in His own body on the tree, that we, being dead to sins, should live for righteousness: by whose stripes you were healed."

Past tense, 'You were healed.' Jesus paid it all for your total deliverance–spirit, soul, and body!

Peter had learned about suffering from Jesus. He knew that Jesus' suffering was part of God's plan (Matthew 16:21-23; Luke 24:25-27, 44-47) and was intended to save us (Matthew 20:28; Matthew 26:28). He also knew that all who follow Jesus must be prepared to suffer (Mark 8:34-35). Peter learned these truths from Jesus and passed them on to us.

Christ died for our sins, in our place, so we would not have to suffer the punishment we deserve. This is called substitutionary atonement.

Psalm 103:2-3 (KJV); "[2]Bless the Lord, O my soul, and forget not all His benefits: [3]Who forgiveth all thine iniquities; who heals all thy diseases."

Notice it doesn't say some, it means all! It also states that healing is one of the benefits that belong to the believer along with the benefit of having our sin forgiven.

3 John 2 (KJV); "Beloved, I wish above all things that thou mayest prosper and be in health, even as thy soul prospereth."

John was concerned for Gaius's physical and spiritual well-being. This was the opposite of the famous heresy that taught the separation of spirit and matter and despised the physical side of life. Today, many people still fall into this way of thinking. This non-Christian attitude logically leads to one of two responses: neglect of the body and physical health, or indulgence of the body's sinful desires. God is concerned for both your body and your soul. As a responsible Christian, you should neither neglect nor indulge yourself, but care for your physical needs and discipline your body so that you are at your best for God's service.

Jeremiah 17:14 (KJV); "Heal me, O LORD, and I shall be healed; save me, and I shall be saved: for thou art my praise."

Jeremiah sees that healing is a finished work along with salvation, paid for at the same time with the same healing blood; then you can get excited about this verse saying, "You did it, Lord, for me." Then, according to this verse, I will agree and say, "I will have healing just as I have salvation; it's mine NOW!"

'Notes'

⇦⇦⇦ Blank page added for 'Notes.'

Blank page added for 'Notes.'

CHAPTER 5

HOW DO WE RECEIVE HEALING?

You will never grow spiritually by confessing what you cannot do. Learn to make your testimony declare what you can do, according to what God said in His Word, and you will begin to grow spiritually. Paul said, "I can do all things through Christ to strengthen this me."—Philippians 4:13 (KJV).

Paul never spoke of what he could not do, but of what he could do. Believe that you can do everything God says you can do. Believe that you are what God says you are. We are more than conquerors through Him that loved us. We are victors. We are conquerors. We always win out when we believe God's Word. If God was with Moses, He will be with us. When God promised to be with Joshua even as He had been with Moses, God meant that He would be with us just as He had been with Moses.

Moses, Daniel, David, Elijah, Peter, and Paul were made of the same material we're made of. They were ordinary people like you and me. Elijah was a man subject to the same passions as we are. Men and women who have been examples of God in other generations were ordinary people just like you and me. They yielded their lives to God, believed His Word, and

acted on them. This is precisely what you can do, and when you do, you will realize the same results.

Health Will Be Restored

Mark 11:24 "Therefore I say to you whatever things you ask when you pray, believe that you receive them, and you will have them." Surely this includes healing!

Most Christians are unaware that our Heavenly Father strongly desires for us to be healed and that Jesus our Lord paid the price for us to be healed. Healing for the body and soul were provided for in the Old Testament, and it was prophesized in the Old Testament that healing would be provided for in the New Testament by the stripes on Jesus' back.

Sometimes when you are still a babe in Christ, God will heal and do many things for you because you are still a babe. But as you get older in the Lord, we are expected to grow up, developing our faith through study and learning to trust God.

The book of Hebrews says, "But without faith, *it is* impossible to please *Him*, for he who comes to God must believe that He is, and *that* He is a rewarder of those who diligently seek Him."—Hebrews 11:6 (NKJV).

Jesus in all four gospels (Matthew, Mark, Luke, and John) would ask a person "What do you want?" After the person spoke what he or she believed Jesus could

do, they received their healing. Paul's words agree with what Jesus said in Romans 10:17. Jesus said that faith comes by hearing (the Word), believing the Word, and speaking forth the Word, through the mouth. Read Romans 10 to understand this fully.

A Sample Prayer

Dear Lord Jesus, I thank you for paying the price for my healing, by the stripes on your back. Thank you for loving me that much. I ask you to let your healing virtue flow from the top of my head to the tip of my toes and heal my (Name the condition by name). Thank you, Father, in Jesus name. Amen!

'Notes'

Blank page added for 'Notes.'

CHAPTER 6

FAITH IS ACTIVATED BY YOUR ACTION

Acting on God's Word justifies your faith. Act on God's Word because faith without works (corresponding action) is dead. James 2:20 (KJV); "But wilt thou know, O vain man, that faith without works is dead?" This Scripture means that we have only as much faith as we demonstrate by our action. Faith must always act. We must confess our faith and act upon our faith if we expect to receive anything from God.

James speaking about Abraham tells us that faith joined with his works, and by his actions, faith was made perfect. "Seest thou how faith wrought with his works, and by works was faith made perfect?"—James 2:22 (KJV).

Faith Put into Action Always Work

James knew that when he wrote: "Even so, faith, if it has not worked, is dead, being alone."—James 2:17 (KJV).

"What *does it* profit, my brethren, if someone says he *[or she]* has faith but does not have works? Can faith save him?"—James 2:14 (NKJV) and, "...Show me

your faith without your works, and I will show you my faith by my works."—James 2:18 (NKJV).

He knew that we must demonstrate our faith by our actions.

Since God could create the worlds with His Words, He indeed can heal your sick body with His Words.

Testimony of Eldon Bollinger #1

In recent years, I believe that God has been teaching me how to receive from Him. I believe that one of the keys is to demonstrate to God that we believe by what we say and do after our praying and believing.

James 2:26 (KJV); "For as the body without the spirit is dead, even so faith without works *[corresponding action]* is dead also." If our faith is dead, it is certain that we will receive nothing from God.

In April of 2008, I was at South Crest Hospital in Tulsa, Oklahoma with a blood disorder. They had removed my spleen which they said would fix the problem. However, it didn't help. In fact, it got worse. They were giving me a medicine that made me very sick and sent me home. They thought that the medication might help, but instead of helping, my body entirely rejected the medicine.

The next morning, after taking the medication, I became violently ill, and my family took me to the

emergency room in Wagoner, Oklahoma. They immediately sent me by ambulance to the Hillcrest Hospital in Tulsa.

We were told that the medicine they had been giving me was the only medicine that could possibly help. After several days in several hospitals, they said there was nothing more than they could do for me and that I would die. Three different doctors from two different hospitals said that to us. I did not believe them, and my family did not believe that I would die.

I have been studying and teaching faith for many years. After praying and asking God to heal me, we quickly began to confess that I was healed. We believed in our hearts, confess with our mouth, and we immediately started to thank God that I was healed according to Mark 11:24, although the evidence had not shown up yet. I continued to confess my healing. On the second Sunday in June, as I went to pray for a lady in our church that was very sick. As I laid my hand on her shoulder to pray, the Lord said in my spirit, "I am healing you now."

I know that it does not always happen this way but I was immediately well, and I have never had any symptoms of that illness again. Several weeks later my wife and I went back to the doctor. They ran blood tests on me and said there was absolutely no evidence of the illness. Praise God, Praise God, Praise God!

Testimony of Eldon Bollinger #2

I saw black spots on everything I looked at. Because we were doing a lot of work for AFOL (Apostolic Faith Online) on the Internet, I used my eyes a lot, and the condition was making my work very difficult.

I prayed and asked God to heal my eyes, and I quoted Mark 11:24 to God. At this time it was easy for me to believe that I was healed and to confess with my mouth my healing. When I would wake up in the morning, I would see large black spots.

For several years I had what they called macular degeneration of my eyes. I could see pretty well except there were gaps in anything that I was trying to read or see. I would see large black spots on the wall. Three weeks later to the day, I woke up and looked at the wall; the black spots were gone! I got dressed and went down to the computer, and everything was bright and clear, but Satan doesn't give up easily. In a few minutes, it all came back. I asked the Lord what was happening and He said the devil is trying to take your healing away from you. I began to rebuke Satan and to command him to go in Jesus name. Within three minutes it all cleared up just like turning a knob to clear up a TV picture; everything was bright and clear again. It's now been over a year, and it has never returned, Praise God, Praise God!

We have now seen many wonderful miracles in our ministry and in our church over the last several years,

and in every case, we had to believe in our hearts that God would do just exactly what He said. We had to confess with our mouth that He would do just exactly what He said in Mark 11:24. We had to believe and confess before we could see the evidence. We had to believe and thank Him for our healing after we prayed before the evidence of healing showed up. We must show God that we believe by what we say and do after we have prayed (I believe that this is one of the primary keys to our receiving anything from God). I also think that we should tell everyone we see that our Lord has healed us before the evidence appears. This demonstrates to God that we believe.

John 20:29 (KJV); "Jesus saith unto him, Thomas, because thou hast seen me, thou hast believed: blessed are they that have not seen, and yet have believed."

Believing God with Our Heart

You see, many people are trying to believe God with their physical senses or with natural, human faith. And if their physical senses tell them their prayer hasn't been answered, then they believe their physical senses instead of the Word of God.

But what do your physical senses have to do with the Bible? God's Word is so, whether it looks like it is so or not. God's Word is true all the time regardless of your senses or feelings. No matter what the circumstance, God's Word is still true.

Faith can't get any clearer. Put your faith in what the Word says rather than in what your senses tell you. You must understand that faith is <u>you</u> believing that God is who He says He is and that God will do what He says He will do. As you do, eventually your mind will be renewed with the Word and the light will come to you.

Romans 8:11 (KJV); "But if the Spirit of him that raised up Jesus from the dead dwell in you, He that raised up Christ from the dead shall also quicken *[make alive]* your mortal bodies by his Spirit that dwelleth in you."

Testimony of Eldon Bollinger #3

On Wednesday, January 6, 2010, I went to the office around 8:00AM. No one else was there. I soon became very ill, and soon noticed that my left side was going numb. A little later, the left side of my face became numb and wrinkled and began to draw. The phone rang, and I realized that I couldn't talk so that anyone could understand me. I had a small stroke, and I knew that I was having all of the symptoms of a major stroke.

I prayed and believed that I was healed. Kathy came into the office, and while we talked a few minutes, I kept my face turned away so she couldn't see my face. She left without realizing that I was sick. I believed that I was healed and I felt that I must demonstrate it to God by what I did and said. I had told Wanell (my wife) that I would go to the store and get her some things that she

needed to prepare food for a funeral dinner. I decided to go to the store and to try not to tell anyone my problem or attract any attention (we live in a small town, and we know most everyone). To make it short, let me say, I went in, got the food, took it home and got back to the office without anyone noticing my condition. All of the time I continued to thank God for my healing. By the time I got back to the office, I was feeling much better, and I could talk. Within about an hour, it was all gone. I was completely healed. I tell everyone that will listen to what my God has done for me.

No one can really understand how grateful and thankful that I am for God's loving care. Most men who at my age (78 at that time) that have a major stroke do not survive and if they do, they are not in good condition afterward.

One thing that I did is that I prayed this prayer from Psalm 103:1-5 almost every day and sometimes several times a day. I firmly believe it helped me and will help you also!

Psalm 103:1-5 (KJV)
1. "Bless the LORD, O my soul: and all that is within me, bless his holy name."
2. "Bless the LORD, O my soul, and forget not all his benefits:"
3. "Who forgiveth all thine iniquities; who healeth all thy diseases;"

4. "Who redeemeth thy life from destruction; who crowneth thee with lovingkindness and tender mercies;"

5. "Who satisfieth thy mouth with good things; so that thy youth is renewed like the eagle's."

'Notes'

⇦⇦⇦   Blank page added for 'Notes.'

Blank page added for 'Notes.'

CHAPTER 7

GOD'S WORD IS THE SEED

Jesus' Words are seed. It is the seed of our divine life. As you seek healing, you must fully understand that it is God's Will for your healing and that understanding must come from God's Word, from hearing, or seeing, or reading God's Word (faith does not come from man's words). It is God's Word that is alive and producing faith.

You cannot reap a harvest of healing without sowing the seeds of God's Word. If no seed has been planted, there will be no harvest of healing or anything else. The sick person must know that it is God's Will to heal him. This is the seed that must be planted in his mind and heart. Even a sinner cannot be saved until he knows that it is God's Will to save him. It is the Word of God that must be planted and watered and fully trusted. This will bring healing to both body and soul. The seed must remain planted and be kept watered before it can produce its harvest. You water and nurture the seed planted by your confession, thanksgiving, praise, worship, and actions.

Proverbs 4:20-22 (KJV); "[20-]My son, attend to my words; incline thine ear unto my sayings. [21-]Let them not depart from thine eyes; keep them in the midst of

thine heart. [22]For they are life unto those that find them, and health to all their flesh."

The Word of God is life and health to only those that find them. If you desire to receive health and healing from God, take time to see the Scriptural promises that promise these results.

If you expect to receive from God, you must pay careful attention to His Words, and you must keep your eyes focused on God's promises, and you must keep them in the midst of thine heart. You must walk by faith, not by sight.

Health to All Our Flesh

Proverbs 4:20-22 (KJV)
20. "My son, attend to my words; incline thine ear unto my sayings.
21. Let them not depart from thine eyes; keep them in the midst of thine heart.
22. For they are life unto those that find them, and health to all their flesh."

Psalm 103:1-5 (KJV)
1. "Bless the LORD, O my soul: and all that is within me, bless his holy name.
2. Bless the LORD, O my soul, and forget not all his benefits:
3. Who forgiveth all thine iniquities; who healeth all thy diseases;

4. Who redeemeth thy life from destruction; who crowneth thee with lovingkindness and tender mercies;

5. Who satisfieth thy mouth with good things; so that thy youth is renewed like the eagle's."

'Notes'

Blank page added for 'Notes.'

CHAPTER 8

ALL CHRISTIANS POSSESS
GOD'S CREATIVE POWER

God is a faith God, and God is a spirit being, and we are 'Spirit Beings' capable of operating in the same level of faith as God. According to God's Word, we can operate with the same creative power that He uses.

Christian's confessions rule them. Victorious Christians know and confess God's Word over their lives and everything that they do. Christianity is called the great confession. Christians who are defeated in life <u>are</u> defeated because they say and believe the wrong things. They continually confess doubt, unbelief and the words of Satan. Proverbs 6:2 (KJV) tells us, "Thou art snared with the words of thy mouth, thou art taken with the words of thy mouth."

God spoke the worlds into being. Listen to what He tells us. Mathew 17:20 (KJV) says, "And Jesus said unto them, Because of your unbelief: for verily I say unto you, If ye *[you]* have faith as a grain of mustard seed, ye shall say unto this mountain, Remove hence to yonder place; and it shall remove; and nothing shall be impossible unto you."

Without faith, it is impossible to please God. Faith-filled words, in line with God's Word, will make you successful every time. Words of doubt and fear will defeat you every time. Your words and God's Words have creative power. Your words can make your life blessed beyond expression, or your words can destroy your life. Your words have creative power, good or bad.

Mark 11:23 (KJV); "For verily I say unto you, That whosoever shall say unto this mountain, Be thou removed, and be thou cast into the sea; and shall not doubt in his heart, but shall believe that those things which he saith shall come to pass; he shall have whatsoever he saith."

Can there be any doubt? Your life is in your mouth (words). Always confess God's Word, even in apparent defeat. Always confess victory in the face of apparent disaster. Confess abundance in the face of great lack; you have creative power.

Just as there is creative power in God's Words spoken by Christians, there is also power in Satan's words spoken by Christians. Never speak negative, critical, doubt or unbelief. It will destroy your life. Christians often speak Satan's words and thereby destroy their own inheritance, by their confession of doubt, fear, and unbelief.

We must learn to speak God's Word. God's Word is powerless when unspoken, but when spoken in faith it will move heaven and earth.

Dr. Charles Capps tells of a time when God spoke to him and said; "I have told my people they can have what they say and they are saying what they have." He also said, "This is a very simple truth, but oh how profound and far-reaching. For as long as you say what you have, you will have what you say, then you, again say what you have, and it will produce no more than what you say."

You can see that you have set a spiritual law in motion that will confine you to the very position or circumstance you are in when you set the law in motion. It is an age-old problem of not looking beyond what you can see with the physical eyes.

A correct application of this spiritual law will change even the most impossible situation. But, to incorrectly apply these laws will hold you in bondage and cause the circumstance to get worse.

Every faith principle, every spiritual law that God has set in His Word was for your benefit. It was designed to put you over in life.

Learn to Release Your Faith in Words

You can have what you say if you learn to release faith from the heart in your words.

Jesus said, "...As thou hast believed, so be it done unto thee."—Matthew 8:13 (KJV). He didn't say it would only work if you believe, right? Whether you believe right, or wrong, it is still the law. "Be not deceived; God is not mocked: for whatsoever a man soweth, that shall he also reap."—Galatians 6:7 (KJV).

This spiritual law is based on the same fundamental principle of seedtime and harvest. The words you speak are seeds that produce after their kind. Just as sure as the words are planted, you can be equally assured a harvest will follow.

Faith talks. When faith talks, it talks faith, not fear or unbelief or doubt.

Jesus said in Mark 11:23 that you can have what you say if what you say comes from faith in your heart.

Mark 11:23 (KJV); "For verily I say unto you, That whosoever shall say unto this mountain, Be thou removed, and be thou cast into the sea; and shall not doubt in his heart, but shall believe that those things which he saith shall come to pass; he shall have whatsoever he saith."

What would happen if Jesus walked down the aisle of your church, laid his hands on the people and said, "It will come to pass that after I have laid my hands on each one of you, everything you say will happen just as you say it?" Half the congregation would jump up and say, "That just tickles me to death." The enemy has so

programmed the minds of people until instead of resisting Him, they have just sort of buddied up with Him and begin to talk his talk.

Train Yourself to Speak God's Word

Let us train ourselves to speak God's Word. Ephesians 5:1 (KJV) tells us to be, "...followers of God, as dear children." The word 'followers' in the Greek language means to 'imitate.' We are to imitate God as a child does his father. If a child imitates his father, he will walk like him, talk like him, and pattern his every move after him.

We Should Do No Less after Our Father, God

When you study the life of Jesus, you find several important facts that caused Him to overcome the world, the flesh, and the devil. I will list a few.

Jesus spent much time in prayer, but He never prayed the problem, He prayed the answer, what God said was the answer.

Jesus spoke accurately, never crooked speech. His conversations always consist of what God said.

Jesus always spoke the end result, not the problem. Never did He confess present circumstances. Jesus spoke the desired results. Jesus also used the written word to defeat Satan.

The Word of God conceived in the heart, formed by the tongue, and spoken out of the mouth has creative power.

Spiritual Law

This is not theory. It is a fact. It is a spiritual law. It works every time that it is applied correctly. God never does anything without saying it first. God is a faith God. God releases His faith in words. "And Jesus answering said unto them, 'Have faith in God.'"—Mark 11:22 (KJV). A more literal translation of the above verse says 'have the God kind of faith, or the faith of God.'

Ephesians 5:1 literally tells us to be imitators of God as children imitate their parents. To imitate God, you must talk like Him and act like Him. He would not ask you to do something you are not able to do.

God's creative power is available to you today, what are you going to do with it?

Eldon's Proverbs
And Memory Verses
'Words' — Real Riches

1. Talk health and healing and not sickness.
2. Talk success and not failure.
3. Talk prosperity and not poverty.
4. Talk Jesus and not Satan.

5. Since it is impossible for God to lie, life and death are in the words you say.
6. Our words imprison us or set us free.
7. Our words reveal what is in our hearts.
8. Jesus said: "And all things, whatsoever ye shall ask in prayer, believing, you shall receive."—Matthew 21:22 (KJV).
9. Loving and kind words are a blessing to any home.
10. Words of faith move mountains.
11. Jesus said, "…What things soever ye desire, when ye pray, believe that ye receive them, and ye shall have them."—Mark 11:24(KJV).

'Notes'

Blank page added for 'Notes.'

CHAPTER 9

THE COMMUNION SERVICE

In the communion service, the cup of wine is a type of the blood of Christ, shed for many for the remission of sins. When we partake of it, we rejoice in the fact that our sinful nature has been changed, that we have been re-created and made new, that we are saved. In this way, I discern or understand the Lord's blood.

In the same communion service, the piece of broken bread is a type of the body of Christ, beaten with stripes by which my sicknesses were healed. When I eat the bread, I rejoice in the fact that my sick, weak body has been changed: that it has become bone of his bone, flesh of his flesh, and body of his body. That is the life of Christ has been made manifest in my mortal flesh, that sickness and disease no longer have power over me, that I am healed. In this way, I discern the Lord's body. Many do not understand this today.

Eldon's Proverbs
And Memory Verses
Love-1 — Real Riches

1. "[7]Beloved, let us love one another: for love is of God, and every one that loveth is born of God and knoweth God. [8]He that loveth not knoweth not God; for God is love."—1 John 7-8 (KJV).

2. He that dwelleth in Love dwelleth in God.
3. Love can bring healing to your life, your family, your world.
4. And the God of Love and Peace be with you.
5. Make Love your way of life; then it cannot fail.
6. Let Love rule your work, your play, your home, your life.
7. The fruit of the Spirit is Love.
8. Choose Love way every time.
9. The beautiful ministry of Jesus Christ was accomplished to give us joy and peace and Love. He walked the rugged cobblestones to patiently teach us that in His Father's Love was hope.
10. Love flowers must often be watered with tears and tender care.

His entire life was dedicated to this, and He viewed humanity with a burning desire to deliver them from their problems and burdens. He was seeking no earthly praise, and He ministered through love to all He met. And finally looking down from the cross, He offered forgiveness and eternal life to all. What great love!

'Notes'

⇦ ⇦ ⇦   Blank page added for 'Notes.'

Blank page added for 'Notes.'

CHAPTER 10

THE AUTHORITY OF GOD'S WORD

Let us put aside our reasoning and our head knowledge knowing that, "Because the carnal mind is enmity against God: for it is not subject to the law of God, neither indeed can be."—Romans 8:7 (KJV).

John 1:1-3 (KJV); "[1]In the beginning was the Word, and the Word was with God, and the Word was God. [2]The same was in the beginning with God. [3]All things were made by him; and without him was not anything made that was made."

You cannot separate God from His Word. He is not only in His Word, but He is back of His Word. He linked Himself with His Word, and He made Himself a part of His Word.

Have faith in the Word of God. If you have faith, Jesus said, "…nothing shall be impossible unto you."—Matthew 17:20 (KJV). He said; "If you abide *[live]* in me, and my words abide *[live]* in you, ye *[you]* shall ask what ye *[you]* will *[desire]*, and it shall be done to you."—John 15:7 (KJV). He also said; "If you ask anything in my name, I will do it."—John 14:14 (KJV). Again, "…What things soever ye desire, when you

pray, believe that ye receive them, and ye shall have them."—Mark 11:24 (KJV).

That is why you can pray the prayer of faith and leave the results with God, regardless of circumstances.

On the basis of the Scriptures, we have become what Christ is. We are what He is. We are in Him. He confirmed this when He said, "He *[those]* who believe on me, the works that I do shall he *[they]* do also...."— John 14:12 (KJV). We now have the authority to work the same works that Jesus accomplished, by doing them in his name.

If this is true of our works, then it is true in regard to our standing with God. God has placed us in Christ Jesus: in whom we have redemption.

God sees us in Christ: of his fullness, we have all received. These facts constitute our confession. We think, speak, pray, and act accordingly.

To tell what Satan is doing in your life is to deny what you are in Christ. When you know that you are what Christ says you are, then you act accordingly, confessing what He is made you. This glorified God and His Word when Jesus said in Mark 9:23 (KJV); "If thou canst believe, all things are possible to him that believeth." He meant that all things are possible to the believer. What masters He has made us to be!

Faith

Hebrews 11:1 (KJV); "Now faith is the substance of things hoped for, the evidence of things not seen."

Hebrews 11:3 (KJV); "Through faith we understand that the worlds were framed by the word of God, so that things which are seen were not made of things which do appear."

Hebrews 11:6 (KJV); "But without faith it is impossible to please him *[God]*: for he that cometh to God must believe that he is, and that he is a rewarder of them that diligently seek him."

Matthew 17:20 (KJV); "And Jesus said unto them, Because of your unbelief: for verily I say unto you, If ye have faith as a grain of mustard seed, ye shall say unto this mountain, Remove hence to yonder place; and it shall remove; and nothing shall be impossible unto you."

Luke 6:38 (KJV); "Give, and it shall be given unto you; good measure, pressed down, and shaken together, and running over, shall men give into your bosom. For with the same measure that ye mete withal it shall be measured to you again."

Luke 6:45 (KJV); "A good man out of the good treasure of his heart bringeth forth that which is good; and an evil man out of the evil treasure of his heart

bringeth forth that which is evil: for of the abundance of the heart his mouth speaketh."

When you pray and believe and offer the prayer of faith, you can from that very moment declare yourself healed by the power of God, because the Word says, "And if we know that he hears us, whatever we ask, we know that we have the petitions that we desire of him."—1 John 5:15 (KJV).

'Notes'

⇦⇦⇦   Blank page added for 'Notes.'

Blank page added for 'Notes.'

CHAPTER 11

THE AUTHORITY OF THE BELIEVER

Jesus called the 12 disciples together and gave them power and authority over all devils, and to cure diseases. And He sent them to preach the kingdom of God, and He healed the sick (see Luke 9:1-2). They departed and went through the towns, preaching the gospel, and healing everywhere.

He ordained the 12 disciples that they should be with Him and that He might send them forth to preach and have the power to heal sicknesses, and the cast out devils.

The Words of Jesus are astonishing when accepted as spoken. They are clear, and they are powerful. People were astonished at his doctrine: for His Words are with power.

We must accept the words of our Lord just as He spoke them and as He commanded. We must heal the sick, cast out evil spirits, and even raise the dead.

Jesus Gave His Power to the Believer's

After Peter told the lame man to rise and to walk in Jesus name. He explained in Acts 3:12-13 that it was

~ 69 ~

the power of the risen Christ that did the miracle. But that power was in Peter, and it is promised to every believer according to Acts 2:39.

The fact is that believers today have the same power and authority that Peter had. Every believer today may do the same things that believers did then by acting on Jesus' Words now as they acted on them then.

God used other people in other generations, but this is your day. Now He wants to use you. You are the believer of today. These signs shall follow them that believe. That includes you. These miracles which were disturbing Herod was not taking place at the hands of a risen profit. They were done by those who lived in the day in which Herod lived; ordinary people who had been given the same power that Elijah or Moses or Daniel had.

Victors and Conquerors

Christians can do everything that God and His Son Jesus said you could do. Jesus said, "…They shall lay hands on the sick and they shall recover."—Mark 16:18 (KJV). That is what will happen when you lay hands on the sick, expecting God to keep His Word. Jesus said, "In my name they shall cast out Devils."—Mark 16:17 (KJV). God gave them power and authority over all devils. The Bible says He did. Therefore, when you command a demon to come out of one who is possessed, the demon must obey you, because you believe and expect God to keep His Word.

If Jesus meant anything, He meant what He said. If the Word of God means anything, it means what it says. God will do what He said He would do, and we can do what God says we can do.

'Notes'

Blank page added for 'Notes.'

CHAPTER 12

YOU HAVE THE AUTHORITY

Luke 9:1-2 (KJV)
1. "Then he called his twelve disciples together, and gave them power and authority over all devils, and to cure diseases.
2. And he sent them to preach the kingdom of God, and to heal the sick."

Luke 9:6 (KJV); "And they departed, and went through the towns, preaching the gospel, and healing everywhere."

Mark 3:14-15 (KJV)
14. "And he ordained twelve, that they should be with him, and that he might send them forth to preach,
15. And to have power to heal sicknesses, and to cast out devils."

Ephesians 1:17-23 (KJV)
17. "That the God of our Lord Jesus Christ, the Father of glory, may give unto you the spirit of wisdom and revelation in the knowledge of him:
18. The eyes of your understanding being enlightened; that ye may know what is the hope of his calling, and what the riches of the glory of his inheritance in the saints,

19. And what is the exceeding greatness of his power to us-ward who believe, according to the working of his mighty power,
20. Which he wrought in Christ, when he raised him from the dead, and set him at his own right hand in the heavenly places,
21. Far above all principality, and power, and might, and dominion, and every name that is named, not only in this world, but also in that which is to come:
22. And hath put all things under his feet, and gave him to be the head over all things to *[for]* the church, [For the benefit of the church.]
23. Which is his body, the fullness of him that filleth all in all."

Ephesians 2:5-6 (KJV)
5. "Even when we were dead in sins, hath quickened *[made alive]* us together with Christ, (by grace ye are saved ;)
6. And hath raised us up together, and made us sit together in heavenly places in Christ Jesus."

   Please note, and set Him at his own right hand in the heavenly places (Ephesians 1:20) and hath raised us up together (Ephesians 2:6). God sees this that we were raised when Christ was raised. When Christ sat down, we sit down too, in the heavenly places; that is where we now are. Now we are seated with Him with all the authority that's given unto Him. That authority belongs to us. We exercise the authority that was given to Him because it belongs to us through the Lord Jesus Christ.

Then we are to help Him carry out His work on the earth using that authority.

Matthew 28:18-20 (KJV)
18. "And Jesus came and spake unto them, saying, All power is given unto me in heaven and in earth.
19. Go ye therefore, and teach all nations, baptizing them in the name of the Father, and of the Son, and of the Holy Ghost:
20. Teaching them to observe all things whatsoever I have commanded you: and, lo, I am with you always, even unto the end of the world. Amen."

Ephesians 6:12 (KJV); "For we wrestle not against flesh and blood, but against principalities, against powers, against the rulers of the darkness of this world, against spiritual wickedness in high places."

The Lord Jesus Christ is seated at the right hand of God the Father, and we are seated there too, far above all of these wicked powers. We are told that we have been given power and authority over all these wicked and evil spirits. God's Word says us to conquer the devil, and He expects us to do that.

Mark 16:15-20 (KJV)
15. "And he said unto them, Go ye into all the world, and preach the gospel to every creature.
16. He that believeth and is baptized shall be saved; but he that believeth not shall be damned.

17. And these signs shall follow them that believe; In my name shall they cast out devils; they shall speak with new tongues;

18. They shall take up serpents; and if they drink any deadly thing, it shall not hurt them; they shall lay hands on the sick, and they shall recover.

19. So then after the Lord had spoken unto them, he was received up into heaven, and sat on the right hand of God.

20. And they went forth, and preached everywhere, the Lord working with them, and confirming the word with signs following. Amen."

But God who is rich in mercy for His great love where when He loved us, that in the ages to come He might show the exceeding riches of His grace and His kindness towards us through our Lord and Savior Jesus Christ. Please notice He says the exceeding greatness of His power toward us who believe. In other words, there is such a putting forth of the divine omnipotence of God's Power through Jesus in raising Him from the dead which is actually the mightiest works of God.

The raising of Jesus from the dead has been opposed by the tremendous powers of Satan. Scripture says all principalities, powers, might, and dominions and every name that is named in the world and the ages to come have endeavored to defeat this plan of God. But Jesus Christ arose anyway; He ascended and is seated at the right hand of the Father. Satanic powers have been baffled and overthrown by the Lord Jesus Christ. He

has been enthroned far above them, ruling with the authority of the most high.

This authority is found in the resurrection and seating of the Lord Jesus Christ by God Himself. He tells us of the exceeding greatness of His power, to us who believe. God is saying this so that the eyes of the church and the believers might be open so that we can understand that Satan is defeated and the believer has power and authority over him and all of his evil forces.

God wants His children to know what is happening. He wants us to know that He set Jesus far above all principalities, and powers, and might, and dominion. The Church as the body of Christ often overlooks this. The spirit of God prayed through Paul so that the church at Ephesus would see this. But God desires that we too should have this wisdom and revelation also.

1 John 3:8 (KJV); "...For this purpose the Son of God was manifested, that he might destroy the works of the devil." Let's now look at Colossians 2:15 (KJV); "And having spoiled principalities and powers, he made a shew [show] of them openly, triumphing over them in it."

The Scriptures seem to tell us Jesus has destroyed the works of the devil, spoiled his power, and utterly defeated him. Since Satan's works and power both have been destroyed; he has become a defeated and destroyed foe.

Jesus' victory was our victory. He did nothing for Himself; He did it all for us. He defeated Satan for us. He spoiled his power for us. He destroyed his works for us. He conquered him for us, and He gave us power and authority over all the works of Satan.

We cannot afford to let Satan defeat and walk on us any longer. We must arise from his bondage. Confess that we are conquerors. Then be sure we hold fast to our confession of faith without wavering. We must maintain and hold fast to our confession of God's Word. Paul tells us, "For with the heart man *[we]* believeth unto righteousness; and with the mouth confession is made unto salvation."—Romans 10:10 (KJV).

Always remember: confession comes first, then Jesus who is the high priest of our confession, responds by granting the thing we have confessed. There is no such thing as salvation without confession, and there is no such thing as healing without confession. Possession is always confession unto salvation or healing and never possession before confession.

Mark 11:24 (KJV); "…What things soever ye *[you]* desire, when ye pray, believe that ye receive them, and ye shall have them."

Every believer has become a master over Satan. We must rise up and do the works that Jesus did when He was here on the Earth.

There is power to break disease and sickness in the hearts and lives of men in Jesus' name. Can the name of Jesus keep us from sickness? Can it keep us from want? Can it keep us from poverty, fear, and the dread of hunger and cold? And can Jesus' name be used just as Jesus suggested in Mark 16:17-18 (KJV)? "[17]And these signs shall follow them that believe; In my name shall they cast out devils; they shall speak with new tongues; [18]They shall take up serpents; and if they drink any deadly thing, it shall not hurt them; they shall lay hands on the sick, and they shall recover."

In the early church, it was utterly independent of circumstances. It didn't mean the whole church; it means the apostles who fully understood the use of the name of Jesus. Men could be sick then by broken fellowship and because of a lack of knowledge, just as they can be today.

The early church that is the Gentile portion of it had never had any revelation from God. It was utterly new raw material. The Jews were in worse condition. They were covenant breakers, as the modern churches are today.

The most difficult to deal with today are the most religious. If there was sickness in the early church, it was to be expected, because they had no precedent, no example ahead of them. Jesus came to destroy the works of the devil. We are His instrument to do His work.

We are to destroy sickness in the church. Our new slogan is 'No more sickness in the body of Christ.'

His Word is to become a reality in the lives of man. The fact that He bore our sins and took sin away by the sacrifice of Himself, and that He made provision for the remission of all we have ever done or said, proves that we should not be sick or in bondage to sin.

He made the sacrifice for sin, the things we have done as a result of the sin nature. The new birth wipes out everything we have ever done.

2 Corinthians 5:17 (KJV); "Therefore if any man is in Christ, he is a new creature *[creation]*: old things are passed away; behold, all things are become new."

Romans 8:1 (KJV) becomes a reality; "There is therefore now no condemnation to them which *[that]* are in Christ Jesus...." The people who are in Christ Jesus are sin free, disease-free, condemnation free.

Let us then arise, take our place, and go out and carry this message of deliverance and victory to others.

It is very important that we grasp clearly 1 John 5:13 (NKJV); "These things I have written to you who believe in the name of the Son of God, that you may know that you have eternal life, and that you may *continue to* believe in the name of the Son of God." We have God's nature which gives us a perfect fellowship with the Father, a perfect right to use His name, a

perfect deliverance and freedom from Satan's dominion.

2 Peter 1:4 (ASV); "Whereby he hath granted unto us his precious and exceeding great promises; that through these ye may become partakers of the *[His]* divine nature."

John 14:14 (ASV); "If ye shall ask anything in my name, that will I do."

Romans 6:14 (ASV); "For sin shall not have dominion over you...."

If sin cannot lord-it (domineer) over you, disease cannot lord-it over you either, because they come from the same source. The nature and life of God that has come into you will give you life and health.

Psalm 91:16 "With long-life I will satisfy him, And show him my salvation." We all admit that the 91st Psalm belongs to the church. It could not apply to the Jews, but it does apply to us.

As it says in Psalm 91:4-7 (NKJV); "[4]He shall cover you with His feathers, And under His wings you shall take refuge; His truth *shall be your* shield and buckler. [5]You shall not be afraid of the terror by night, Nor for the arrow *that* flies by day; [6]*Nor* for the pestilence *that* walks in darkness, *Nor* for the destruction that lays waste at noonday. [7]A thousand shall fall at your side,

~ 81 ~

And ten thousand at your right hand; *but* it shall not come near you."

There is protection from earthquakes, cyclones, from pestilence, from sickness, and much more.

The life in the vine is in the branch. As soon as the branch is wounded, the vine pours life into the wounded branch so it can go on and bear fruit. So the life of God pours into the body of Christ, and He pours life into the church members with sickness, disease, and want, so they can go on and bear fruit to the glory of God.

These things put us into the realm of the supernatural. We are linked up with Christ because He said, "I am the vine, and you are the branches."—John 15:5 (NKJV). So we are victors and conquers and over-comers, and there need be no defeat in the body of Christ.

'Notes'

⇦⇦⇦ Blank page added for 'Notes.'

Blank page added for 'Notes.'

CHAPTER 13

USE YOUR AUTHORITY AND RESIST FEAR

Matthew 18:18 (KJV); "Verily *[Truly, Honestly]* I say unto you, Whatsoever ye *[you]* shall bind on earth shall be bound in heaven: and whatsoever ye *[you]* shall loose on earth shall be loosed in heaven."

The word 'bind' means to forbid. The word 'loose' means to let go or to allow to go free. Do not allow sickness, pain or disease run free in your body. Bind it or forbid it to stay there any longer because of your rights as a believer. Put your foot down and command it to leave in the Name of Jesus!

John 10:10 (NKJV); "The thief *[Satan]* does not come except to steal, and to kill, and to destroy. I *[Jesus]* have come that they may have life, and that they may have it more abundantly."

Here we see the desired will of the Lord for every believer, that we experience abundant life. According to this verse, He came for this very purpose. We also see that it is not God who afflicts us. The word here for life is the Greek word 'ZOE.' One highly respected commentator describes the true meaning of the word in this verse as: "Life being the highest and best of which Christ is." In light of that meaning, you can easily see

the wonderful gift of life the Lord wants for each of us. Sickness and disease are truly not in His plan for us simply because He has none to give.

Luke 10:19 (KJV); "Behold, I give unto you power [authority] to tread on serpents and scorpions, and over all the power of the enemy: and nothing shall by any means hurt you."

This is an exciting verse as Jesus said he'd given us authoritative power over ALL, not some of the enemy! Command Satan to take his hands off of you. Command sickness and disease to leave you now in the Name of Jesus.

Isaiah 41:10 (NIV); "So do not fear, for I am with you; do not be dismayed, for I am your God. I will strengthen you and help you; I will uphold you with my righteous right hand."

God chose Israel through Abraham because He wanted to, not because the people deserved it (see Deuteronomy 7:6-8 & Deuteronomy 9:4-6). Although God chose the Israelites to represent Him to the world, they failed to do this; so God punished them and sent them into captivity. Now all believers are God's chosen people, and all share the responsibility of representing Him to the world.

One day God will bring all his faithful people together. We need not fear because of the following reasons:

1. God is with us, "...I am with you..."—Isaiah 41:10.
2. God has established a relationship with us, "I am your God"—Isaiah 41:10 and,
3. God gives us assurance of his strength, help, and victory over sin and death.

Have you realized all the ways God has helped you?

Isaiah 54:17 (NKJV); "No weapon formed against you shall prosper, and every tongue *which* rises against you in judgment YOU shall condemn. This *is* the heritage *[birthright]* of the servants of the LORD, and their righteousness *is* from me, says the LORD."

Sickness is judging you falsely; it is your birthright to live in health. You condemn it, with the Word of God, and command it to leave your body.

Psalm 102:19-20 (NKJV); "[19]For He looked down from the height of His sanctuary; From heaven the Lord viewed the earth, [20]To hear the groaning of the prisoner, to release *[loose]* those appointed to death."

If you are born-again, then YOU are not appointed to death but unto life in Christ Jesus. The Word (the Bible) tells us that He who the Son sets free is free indeed (see John 8:36). Take hold of and insist upon your covenant right of freedom today in Jesus Name. Command the devil, sickness, disease, pain, and suffering to GO in Jesus name. You have another appointment with Him, and that appointment is supernatural, overflowing, and abundant life in Jesus

Christ our Lord. You may feel like a prisoner because of your circumstance, but rejoice because God's Will <u>IS</u> to release you from it. Begin to praise Him for it.

1 John 4:4 (KJV); "… greater is he *[GOD]* that is in you, than he *[Satan]* that is in the world."

It is easy to be frightened by the wickedness we see all around us and overwhelmed by the problems we face. Evil is apparently much stronger than we are. John assures us, however, that God is even stronger. He will conquer all evil–and his Spirit and his Word live in our hearts!

1 John 5:4 (KJV); "For whatsoever is born of God overcometh the world: and this is the victory that overcometh the world, even our faith."

Jesus never promised that obeying Him would be easy. But the hard work and self-discipline of serving Christ is no burden to those who love Him. And if our load starts to feel heavy, we can always trust Christ to help us bear it (see Matthew 11:28-30).

John 17:14 (KJV); "I have given them thy word; and the world hath hated them, because they are not of the world, even as I am not of the world."

Jesus states that we as believers are not of the world. Sickness, disease, and failure belong to the world. As a believer, we are given the right to overcome that which comes against us by holding fast to the Word of God.

While we do not deny that the problem or circumstance exists, we do however deny it the right to stay through our faith in God and His Word! Know this: Faith in God is a victory all of the time!

Romans 8:31 (KJV); "What shall we then say to these things? If God be for us, who can be against us?"

You are a winner; you are victorious through the Lord Jesus Christ. Begin to see yourself the way God sees you.

1 John 4:17 (NKJV); "Love has been perfected among us in this: that we may have boldness in the day of judgment; because as He is, so are we in this world."

Not only can we have boldness in the Day of Judgment, but we can have boldness now in this life in the face of adversity, knowing who we are in Christ, knowing what belongs to us in Him and tenaciously holding onto it, refusing what the enemy wants us to have. As above verse says so clearly, "…as He is, so are we in this world." Think about that for a moment, how is He now? He is not sick; He is not diseased–it can't touch Him, and we are His body–the body of Christ. Insist on having the blessing of the Lord manifested in you–praise Him for it now, worship Him!

1 Corinthians 6:15-17 (NKJV); "[15]Do you not know that your bodies are members of Christ? Shall I then take the members of Christ and make *them* members of a harlot? Certainly not! [16]Or do you not know that he

who is joined to a harlot is one body *with her*? For "the two," He says, "shall become one flesh." [17]But he who is joined to the Lord is one spirit *with* Him."

Sickness has no right to Him, so it has no legal right to us. It is illegal, off-limits; it has no right to stay. Take a firm stand and run off the attack and lie of the enemy. You belong to Him (Jesus); you are washed in His precious Blood, the covenant Blood. Command it to leave and insist on your rights now, and don't quit until it changes and becomes just as the Word says it should be!

2 Peter 1:3-4 (NKJV); "[3]As His divine power has given to us all things that *pertain* to life and godliness, through the knowledge of Him who called us by glory and virtue, [4]by which have been given to us exceedingly great and precious promises, that through these you may be partakers of the divine nature, having escaped the corruption that is in the world through lust."

In verse 3, notice the past tense use of 'has given us all things that pertain to life.' The blessing of health was purchased for us at the cross; it belongs to you now. Notice the importance of the Word of God; your healing must be rooted steadfastly on the Word, not on what you see or how you feel. And did you also take note that we are partakers of His divine nature! His nature is total health and well-being, <u>expect it!</u>

1 Corinthians 1:9 (NKJV); "God *is* faithful, by whom you were called into the fellowship of His Son, Jesus Christ our Lord."

The word 'fellowship' is a strong covenant word in the original Greek text. It means intimacy, partnership and participation, and also communion. In other words, because we are born-again, we have been given the right to share intimately, in partnership and participation in His life. Know that He is life, the purest form of life, and He's called us to share intimately in it with Him. It's a place where sickness and disease have no right. This is your birthright, count on it and expect it. And I love how this verse starts out, 'God is faithful.' He's faithful to His Covenant Word, and to His covenant people, He's faithful to YOU!

Romans 5:17 (NKJV); "For if by the one man's offense *[Adam]* death reigned through the one, much more those who receive abundance of grace and of the gift of righteousness will reign in life through the one, Jesus Christ."

I love this verse! Did you notice, it did not say you might or you possibly could, it says you will reign in life (this life in the here and now). Are you reigning in life? If you are not experiencing victory, know that it is a breach of the Word of God for it to remain and become the norm. Get mad, with righteous indignation, and command the circumstances to leave and take hold of the victory that is yours through the Word. For this is the Will of God!

Genesis 1:28 (KJV); "And God blessed them, and God said to them, 'Be fruitful, and multiply, and replenish the earth, and subdue it: and have dominion over the fish of the sea, and over the fowl of the air, and over every living thing that moveth upon the earth."

The red blood cells of your body already obey this verse, as they are being multiplied and replenished every 80-120 days! Look at the rest of what God said to mankind–subdue and have dominion over every living thing! Wow! That includes cancer, bacteria, parasites, viruses and all microorganisms that cause sickness and disease. He gave the blessing; He gave the command, He gave you the right–now do it. Put your foot down on sickness and disease and command it to go–it has no right to stay; you are a blood-bought child of God! Don't put up with it another minute, subdue and take dominion!

Colossians 1:13 (NKJV); "He has delivered us from the power of darkness and conveyed *us* into the kingdom of the Son of His love." NOTE: To be conveyed is to be transferred, removed out of one and placed into another. The power of darkness which includes the curse no longer has a hold on us as we are now members of a different kingdom–the Kingdom of God. There is no sickness and no disease in the Kingdom of God.

Make Jesus the Lord of your life. Reverence Him by closing all doors to the enemy, giving Him first place!

Proverbs 3:7-8 (NKJV); "[7]Do not be wise in your own eyes; Fear the LORD and depart from evil. [8]It will be health to your flesh, and strength to your bones."

The term "Fear the Lord" means to reverence and worship the Lord in all things.

Exodus 15:26 (KJV); "...If thou will diligently harken to the voice of the Lord thy God, and wilt do that which is right in his sight, and wilt give ear to his commandments, and keep all his statutes, I will put *[permit]* none of these diseases upon thee, which I have brought upon the Egyptians: for I am the Lord that healeth thee."

God promised that if the people obeyed Him, they would be free from the diseases that plagued the Egyptians. Little did they know that many of the moral laws He later gave them were designed to keep them free from sickness. For example, following God's Law against prostitution would keep them free of venereal disease. God's Laws for us are often designed to keep us from harm. Men and women are complex human beings. Our physical, emotional, and spiritual lives are intertwined. Modern medicine is now acknowledging what these laws assumed. If we want God to care for us, we need to submit to his directions for living.

Exodus 23:25 "So you shall serve *[worship]* the Lord your God, and He will bless your bread and your water. And I will take sickness away from the midst of you."

If you're in the furnace, it's easy to catch on fire. God warned the Israelites about their neighbors whose beliefs and actions could turn them away from Him. We also live with neighbors whose values may be completely different from ours. We are called to maintain a lifestyle that shows our faith. This can be a struggle, especially if our Christian lifestyle differs from other religious lifestyles. Our lives should show that we put obeying God before doing what is praised and accepted by society.

True worship from the heart is a key to walking in divine health bringing forth humility of heart. Close every door to the devil that you are aware of. Take time each day to worship and love God from your heart.

Psalm 91:9-10 (KJV); "[9]Because thou hast made the LORD, which is my refuge, even the most High, thy habitation; [10]There shall no evil befall thee, neither shall any plague come nigh thy dwelling."

Malachi 4:2-3 (NKJV); "[2]But to you who fear *[reverence, worship]* My name, The Sun of Righteousness shall arise With healing in His wings; and you shall go out *[forth]*, and grow fat *[up]* like stall-fed calves. [3]You shall trample the wicked, For they shall be ashes under the soles of your feet on the day that I do *this*," Says the Lord of hosts."

Know that when you ask the Lord for healing, it is already His Will and He hears you, and He agrees.

Know He has already settled it in the atonement of the blood of Jesus Christ, He says "YES!"

Psalm 30:2 (KJV); "O LORD my God, I cried unto thee, and thou hast healed me."

Psalm 107:19-20 (KJV); "[19]Then they cry unto the LORD in their trouble, and he saveth them out of their distresses. [20]He sent his word, and healed them, and delivered them from their destructions."

Most people who come and ask for healing are healed as far as God is concerned. The main problem is to keep these people from the influence of unbelief, from skepticism, and those who are slaves to the sense knowledge; we must not look at circumstances. It's essential to keep people in God's Word even after the evidence of healing has shown up and not to associate with unbelievers.

Satan tempted the Lord Jesus Christ; he tempts every individual that has been saved, and he will tempt every person who has been healed. Don't allow him to bring doubt and unbelief into your life once you are healed. Most new Christian converts are encouraged to resist temptation, and the devil, and to look to Christ. The person who is healed will often be given suggestions by friends and foes, by the weak and the well, by the preacher and church members not to be too sure of healing, and to be on the alert for the return of the old affliction. God will always do what He said He would do when it is said in faith.

Those who have been healed should be taught that it is God's Plan that sickness should be taken from their midst (Exodus 23:25) and that God's Will is that they should prosper and be in health, even as their soul prospers (see 3 John 2:2).

These promises will be fulfilled in the lives of those who boldly proclaim it and believe it.

Our Lord Jesus Christ suffered all the sickness and pain that you have right now. He did it for you, and He will heal your physical infirmities and diseases when you ask Him to. He watches over His Word to perform it and when He said, "...I am the Lord thy God that healeth thee."—Exodus 15:26 (KJV), we can know that we are healed.

You do not have to try to believe, just act on The Word. Acting is believing. Do not make a confession that contradicts what God has said. Make your testimony and your confession agree with God's Word regardless of the circumstances. Keep His Word coming out of your mouth. God will always do what He said He would do.

Do not talk doubt and unbelief. Learn to quote the Scriptures continually, and they will become yours, they will be deposited in your heart, and they will come forth as you need them. Do not talk sickness and pain, talk about your healing and what God is doing for you. When you talk about sickness, you magnifying and glorify the devil whom you admit by your words is able

to make you sick. Make Satan listen to your praise of God and your conversation about the Living Word in the promises of God. While Jesus was being tempted, He defeated Satan by saying "It is written," and then by repeating his Father's Words. You can defeat Satan the same way.

'Notes'

Blank page added for 'Notes.'

CHAPTER 14

BELIEVE & CONFESS

Believe in your heart and confess with your mouth. Romans 10:9-10 tells us that we must believe in our heart and confess with our mouth when we accept Jesus Christ as our Lord and Savior, and when we do, we will become sons or daughters of Almighty God.

Healing is very much the same way. When we pray and ask the Lord to heal us, we must believe in our heart and confess with your mouth that He has healed us.

You must demonstrate your faith by what you say and do. Faith without corresponding action is not real faith at all.

Always remember, confession comes first and then Jesus, who is the high priest of our confession, responds by granting the thing we have confessed.

Our confession causes the high priest of our confession to grant us what we believe with our heart that we have, and this brings us into possession of it. That is faith. God is a faith God. That is to say; He is a God who requires faith. We received from God only the things we believe we receive.

Mark 11:24 (KJV); "…What things soever things you desire, when you pray, believe that you receive them, and you shall have them."

People sometimes claim to have great faith. That may be true, but with all of the faith in the world not accompanied by the corresponding action, is a dead faith. "…that faith without works is dead?"—James 2:20 (KJV). It is possible to have faith and yet receive nothing from God.

When you say you believe, that is a different thing because the word 'believe' is a verb and a verb is an action word. If you believe, that means you are acting on God's promise; and when you couple action with faith, that is believing. You're acting on God's promise always puts Him to work bringing about the fulfillment of a promise. Believing the Word means acting on the Word. Believing is acting; faith is the cause or result of this action.

When we demonstrate our faith by what we say and do, it will bring the answer every time.

When you ask the Lord to heal you, you know that He will, because He said that He would. Jesus said, "If you ask anything in my name, I will do it."—John 14:14 (KJV). Anything includes healing or any other need.

1 Peter 2:24 (KJV); "…by whose stripes ye [you] were healed." Does that include you? Exodus 15:26 (KJV); "…I am the Lord that he healeth thee." Does

that include you? Psalm 103:3 (KJV); "…who healeth all thy diseases." Does that include you?

James 5:14-15 (KJV); "[14-]Is any sick among you? Let him call for the elders of the church; and let them pray over him, anointing him with oil in the name of the Lord: [15-]And the prayer of faith shall save the sick, and the Lord shall raise him up; and if he has committed sins, they shall be forgiven him." Does that include you?

Do you believe that God's promises are for you? If you do, you need to claim them and confess them as yours. Do not doubt, only believe. In the Scriptures, God is speaking directly to you, so believe.

Confession brings possession. Always remember: confession comes first, and then Jesus, who is the high priest of our confession, responds by granting the thing we have confessed. There is no such thing as salvation without confession. There is no such thing as healing without confession. It is always confession to healing, never possession before confession.

Our confession is essential; it causes the high priest of our confession (Jesus) to grant us what we believe with our heart that we have, and that brings us into possession of it. This is the way our faith works. God is a faith God. That is to say; He is a God who requires faith. We receive from God only the things we believe we receive and confess for always remember Mark 11:24 (KJV); "…What things soever ye desire, when ye

pray, believe that ye receive them, and ye shall have them." Confession is faith's way of expressing itself in our testimony.

Paul declares that he preached the word of faith then he told us that the word of faith must be in our hearts and in our mouth. Your confession needs to be in line with God's Word

God will always make His Word good. Learn to confess what our Lord says, and He will fulfill his promise to you because He is the high priest of our confession. The confessions of 'I am the Lord that heals you,' and 'by his stripes, I'm healed' always follows the manifestation of healing. Just as the confession of Jesus as Lord and Savior all always follows the experience of salvation.

Jesus is the high priest of our confession, our words, and what we say with our lips when it corresponds to His Word. He does according to what He says. We should never confess anything but victory because Paul says; "...in all these things we are more than conquerors...."—Romans 8:37 (KJV).

The Bible contains God's last Will and Testament, in which He bequeathed to us all of the blessings of the redemption. Since healing is in His Will for us; to say that God is not willing to heal us all as His Will states so clearly, would be to change the Will. Jesus is not only the testator (made a will) who died, but He was resurrected and is also the mediator of the Will. He is

our advocate, and He will not beat us out of our inheritance.

There is no better way to know the Will of God than by reading the Gospels (Scriptures), which record the teachings and the works of Christ. Jesus was the physical expression of the Father's Will. His life was both a revelation and a manifestation of the unchanging Love and Will of God. He acted out the Will of God for us. When Jesus laid his hands on every one of them and healed them, He was revealing and doing the Will of God for all people.

Hebrews 10:7 (KJV); "…Lo, I come to do your will, O God."

Everything Jesus did for needy humanity during his earthly ministry was a direct revelation of the perfect Will of God for the human race. "For I came down from heaven, not to do my own will, but the will of him that sent me."—John 6:38 (KJV).

The benefits of redemption are for you. If God healed all then, He still heals all; that is, all that come to Him for healing.

"Jesus Christ *is* the same yesterday, today, and forever."—Hebrews 13:8 (NKJV).

"And great multitudes followed Him, and He healed them all."—Matthew 12:15 (NKJV).

All those who touched Him were made perfectly whole (Matthew 14:36).

The whole multitude sought to touch Him, and He healed them all.

Luke 4:40 (KJV); "Now when the sun was setting, all that had any sick with divers *[various]* diseases brought them unto him; and he laid his hands on every one of them, and healed them."

Acts 8:6-8 (KJV); "[6-]And the people with one accord gave heed unto those things which Philip spake, hearing and seeing the miracles which he did. [7-]For unclean spirits, cried with a loud voice, come out of many that were possessed with them: and many with palsies *[paralysis]*, and that were lame, were healed. [8-]And there was great joy in that city."

Faith cannot be exercised when one is undecided as to whether or not God will heal all. Let it be a settled fact: it is God's Will to heal you. You have a right to healing as well as forgiveness when you believe. God said; "…I'm the Lord who healed you (Exodus 15:26). If God said this, and God cannot lie, He meant it. What God says is true. So, healing is yours.

Healing is part of the gospel and is to be preached throughout the entire world and to every creature, to the end of the world. Being part of the gospel, the divine blessing of physical healing is for all.

⇦⇦⇦   Blank page added for 'Notes.'

Blank page added for 'Notes.'

CHAPTER 15

THE GIFT OF HEALING

Romans 11:29 (NKJV); "For the gifts and the calling of God are irrevocable."

He's the giver of gifts. He doesn't take them back; they cannot be canceled!

Philippians 2:13 (NKJV); "For it is God who works in you both to will and to do for *His* good pleasure."

What do we do when we don't feel like obeying? God has not left us alone in our struggles to do His Will. He wants to come alongside us and be with us to help. God helps us want to obey Him and then gives us the power to do what He wants. The secret to a changed life is to submit to God's control and let Him work. Next time, ask God to help you want to do His Will.

To be like Christ, we must train ourselves to think like Christ. To change our desires to be more like Christ's, we need the power of the indwelling spirit (see Philippians 1:19), the influence of faithful Christians, obedience to God's Word (not just exposure to it), and sacrificial service. Often it is in doing God's Will that

we gain the desire to do it (see Philippians 4:8-9). Do what He wants and trust Him to change your desires.

Matthew 11:28 (Amp); "Come to Me, all who are weary and heavily burdened, and I will give you to rest."

The word 'rest' here literally means to cease from toil or labor in order to recover and collect his/her strength. It implies a feeling of wholeness and well-being. Place your focus on Jesus and all He has purchased for you. Take the focus off of the circumstances, and begin praising Him for all that He has done for you. You are highly favored by God–He's given it all to you. Spend time each day just loving (on) God. Come to Him through intimate worship, and experience this rest.

Deuteronomy 29:29 (AMP); "The secret things belong to the Lord our God, but the things which are revealed *and* disclosed belong to our children and to us forever, so that we may do all the words of this law."

This Scripture makes it so clear that healing and health belong to you and your posterity–family line. Healing has been revealed to us through the Word of God and declared to us through the shed covenant Blood of Jesus Christ on the cross. Every Scripture on this page is declaring your revealed covenant right. Dig in and take hold of it by faith and refuse to let go of your birthright!

James 1:17 (KJV); "Every good gift and every perfect gift is from above, and cometh down from the Father of lights, with whom is no variableness, neither shadow of turning."

Healing is a wonderful gift from God, and here again is another proof He does not change. What God did yesterday, He will do again today–Praise the Lord for He is still the Healer!

1 Corinthians 3:21-22 (NKJV); "21-Therefore let no one boast in men. For all things are yours: 22-whether Paul or Apollos or Cephas, or the world or life or death, or things present or things to come—all are yours."

The above verses say it so clear that the Lord is holding nothing back from us. Healing is included in the claim of 'all things' and certainly, is included in the word 'life.' Begin to praise the Lord for your healing which is a gift to you from the Lord, and the manifestation that will come as you receive the promise by faith.

James 5:14-15 (NKJV); "14-Is any sick among you? Let him call for the elders of the church; and let them pray over him, anointing him with oil in the name of the Lord: 15-And the prayer of faith shall save the sick, and the Lord shall raise him up. And if he has committed sins, they shall be forgiven him."

James is referring to someone who is incapacitated physically. In Scripture, oil was both a medicine (see the parable of the Good Samaritan in Luke 10:30-37)

and a symbol of the Spirit of God (as used in anointing kings, see 1 Samuel 16:1-13). Therefore, oil can represent both the medical and the spiritual spheres of life. Christians should not separate the physical and the spiritual–Jesus Christ is Lord of both the body and the spirit.

People in the Church are not alone. Members of Christ's body should be able to count on others for support and prayer, especially when they are sick or suffering. The elders should be on call to respond to the illness of any member. The Church should stay alert to pray for the needs of all its members.

Matthew 8:2 (NIV); "A man with leprosy came and knelt before him and said, 'Lord, if you are willing, you can make me clean.'"

Matthew 8:3 (NIV); "Jesus reached out his hand and touched the man. 'I am willing,' he said, 'Be clean!' Immediately he was cured of his leprosy."

Mark 1:40 (NIV); "A man with leprosy came to him and begged him on his knees, 'If you are willing, you can make me clean.'"

Mark 1:41 (NIV); "Jesus was indignant *[showing anger]* reached out his hand to the man. 'I am willing,' he said, 'be clean!' Immediately Jesus healed the sick person."

It is still His Will to heal people today. Jesus Christ is the same yesterday, today, and forever (Hebrews 13:8).

Mark 1:42 (NIV); "Immediately the leprosy left him and he was cured."

Luke 5:12 (NIV); "While Jesus was in one of the towns, a man came along who was covered with leprosy. When he saw Jesus, he fell with his face to the ground and begged him, 'Lord, if you are willing, you can make me clean.'"

Luke 5:13 (NIV); "Jesus reached out his hand and touched the man. 'I am willing,' he said. 'Be clean!' And immediately the leprosy left him."

Jesus was willing to heal the sick back then, and He is still willing to heal the sick today. Notice He did the healing by laying hands on the man and the man's body to be healed. Jesus did not pray for the healing (in the sense of asking God to heal the man). He commanded it. Healing works precisely the same way today.

Mark 1:32 (NIV); "That evening after sunset the people brought to Jesus all the sick and demon-possessed."

Mark 1:33 (NIV); "The whole town gathered at the door."

Mark 1:34 (NIV); "And Jesus healed many who had various diseases. He also drove out many demons, but he would not let the demons speak because they knew who he was."

The people came to Jesus in the evening after sunset. This was the Sabbath (Mark 1:21), their day of rest lasting from sunset Friday to sunset Saturday. The Jewish leaders had proclaimed it was against the law to be healed on the Sabbath (Matthew 12:10; Luke 13:14). The people didn't want to break this law or the Jewish law that prohibited traveling on the Sabbath, so they waited until sunset. After the sun went down, the crowds were free to find Jesus so He could heal them.

Why didn't Jesus want the demons to reveal who He was?

1. By commanding the demons to remain silent, Jesus proved His authority and power over them.
2. Jesus wanted the people to believe He was the Messiah because of what He said and did, not because of the demons' words.
3. Jesus wanted to reveal His identity as the Messiah according to His timetable, not according to Satan's timetable.

Satan wanted the people to follow Jesus around for what they could get out of Him, not because He was the Son of God who could truly set them free from sin's guilt and power.

Luke 4:40 (NKJV); "When the sun was setting, all those who had any that were sick with various diseases brought them to Him; and He laid His hands on every one of them and healed them."

Luke 4:41 (NKJV); "And demons also came out of many, crying out and saying, 'You are the Christ, the Son of God!' And He, rebuking *them*, did not allow them to speak, for they knew He was the Christ."

Over and over Jesus healed the sick people who were brought to Him. It is His Will to heal, then and now. Notice that He did not pray for the demons to leave, He told them not to reveal who He was, and told them to go. He sent them out with a word. Deliverance works just the same way today and is often just as easy as in this passage.

'Notes'

Blank page added for 'Notes.'

CHAPTER 16

HEALING THROUGH GOD'S WORD

Proverbs 4:20-22 (KJV); "²⁰⁻My son, attend to My words; incline thine ear unto my sayings. ²¹⁻Let them not depart from thine eyes; keep them in the midst of thine heart. ²²⁻For they are life unto those that find them, and health *[literally medicine]* to all their flesh."

Here is as plain as it can be: the taking of God's Word is life and medicine to your flesh. <u>So just don't take your prescribed natural medicine alone, add the Word of God along with it. Prescribed medicine can heal and help some things, but God's medicine can heal all.</u>

John 8:32 (KJV); "And ye shall know the truth, and the truth shall make you free."

The Word of God is 'Truth,' see John 17:17. Once you know the truth concerning healing in God's redemptive plan, then you can begin to exercise faith and expect the promises of God to manifest in you–and they will–REJOICE!

Jeremiah 23:29 (KJV); "Is not my word like a fire? saith the LORD, And like a hammer that breaks the rock in pieces?"

The Word of God is an all-consuming fire that will melt away, and burn off that which is not of God. The Word of God is a powerful crushing force to break apart even the toughest and most stubborn circumstances. Continue taking the hammer of God's Word and continue to hit the situations in your life that are not of God, until they give way and become as the Word says they should be. Persistence breaks down resistance!

2 Timothy 3:16-17 (KJV); "[16]All Scripture is given by inspiration of God, and is profitable for doctrine, for reproof, for correction, for instruction in righteousness: [17]That the man of God may be perfect *[complete]*, thoroughly furnished *[equipped]* unto all good works."

Does your body and/or mind need correction? God's Word is just the medicine. According to the above verse, we see that it is His Will that you may be complete and thoroughly equipped for every good work. If you are sick, you cannot do the work of the ministry– know that God wants you to be able-bodied, a living example in every area of His Grace, Mercy, and Power.

John 6:63 (NKJV); "It is the Spirit who gives life; the flesh profits nothing. The words that I speak to you are spirit, and they are life."

God's Word is healing; it will bring health to your flesh (see Proverbs 4:22). That's why it is essential to continue to go over the healing Scriptures daily. Building your faith in the area of healing, imparting the

very life of God into your cells. Fill-up with God's Word!

Psalm 119:50 (KJV); "This is my comfort in my affliction: for thy word has given me life."

The psalmist (author/composer) talks about keeping the laws and yet being free. Contrary to what we often expect, obeying God's Laws does not inhibit or restrain us. Instead, it frees us to be what God designed us to be. By seeking God's salvation and forgiveness, we have freedom from sin and the resulting oppressive guilt. By living God's way, we have the freedom to fulfill God's Plan for our lives.

Romans 10:17 (KJV); "So then faith comes by hearing, and hearing by the Word of God."

Faith for healing comes by hearing God's Word concerning healing. So just as you may be taking medicine two or three times a day, do the same thing with the promises in the Word of God regarding healing and allow your faith to be built up! You'll be amazed at the change that will take place.

John 15:7 (NKJV); "If you abide in Me, and My words abide in you, you will ask what you desire, and it shall be done for you."

Many people try to be good, honest people who do what is right. But Jesus says the only way to live a truly good life is to stay close to Him, like a branch attached

to the vine. Apart from Christ, our efforts are unfruitful. Are you receiving the nourishment and life offered by Christ, the vine? If not, you are missing a special gift He has for you.

Isaiah 55:11 (KJV); "So shall my word be that goeth forth out of my mouth: It shall not return unto me void, but it shall accomplish that which I please, and it shall prosper in the thing whereto I sent it."

God's Word on healing will accomplish healing in you.

Jeremiah 1:12 (KJV); "Thou hast well seen: for I will hasten my word to perform it."

God is looking, searching eagerly for someone to take Him at His Word so He can perform it on their behalf.

The vision of the branch of an almond tree revealed the beginning of God's judgment because the almond tree is among the first to blossom in the spring. God saw the sins of Judah and the nations, and He would carry out swift and certain judgment. The boiling pot tilting away from the north and spilling over Judah, pictured Babylon delivering God's scalding judgment against Jeremiah's people.

The problems we face may not seem as ominous as Jeremiah's, but they are critical to us and may overwhelm us! God's promise to Jeremiah, and to us, is that nothing will defeat him completely; He will help us

through the most agonizing problems. Face each day with the assurance that God will be with you and see you through.

Joshua 21:45 (NKJV); "Not a word failed of any good thing which the LORD had spoken to the house of Israel. All came to pass."

How much more sure is this promise to us since our covenant with God is based on the shed Blood of Jesus Christ!

God proved faithful in fulfilling every promise He had given to Israel. Fulfillment of some promises took several years, but <u>every one was fulfilled.</u> His promises will be fulfilled according to His timetable, not ours. He knows His Word is sure. The more we learn of those promises God has fulfilled and continues to fulfill, the easier it is to hope for those yet to come. Sometimes we become impatient, wanting God to act in a certain way now. Instead, we should faithfully do what we know He wants us to do and trust Him for the future.

Matthew 8:5 (NIV); "Now when Jesus had entered Capernaum, a centurion came to him, asking for help."

The centurion could have let many obstacles stand between him and Jesus–pride, doubt, money, language, distance, time, self-sufficiency, power, and race. But he didn't. If he did not let these barriers block his

approach to Jesus, we don't need to either. What keeps you from Christ?

Matthew 8:6 (KJV); "'Lord,' he said, 'my servant lies at home paralyzed, suffering terribly.'"

Matthew 8:7 (KJV); "And Jesus saith unto him, I will come and heal him."

Matthew 8:8 (KJV); "The centurion answered and said, Lord, I am not worthy that thou shouldest come under my roof: but speak the word only, and my servant shall be healed."

Matthew 8:9 (KJV); "For I am a man under authority, having soldiers under me: and I say to this man, Go, and he goeth; and to another, Come, and he cometh; and to my servant, Do this, and he doeth it."

Matthew 8:10 (KJV); "When Jesus heard it, he marvelled, and said to them that followed, Verily I say unto you, I have not found so great faith, no, not in Israel."

Matthew 8:11 (KJV); "And I say unto you, That many shall come from the east and west, and shall sit down with Abraham, and Isaac, and Jacob, in the kingdom of heaven."

Matthew 8:12 (KJV); "But the children of the kingdom shall be cast out into outer darkness: there shall be weeping and gnashing of teeth."

Matthew 8:13 "And Jesus said unto the centurion, Go thy way; and as thou hast believed, so be it done unto thee. And his servant was healed in the selfsame hour."

A centurion was a career military officer in the Roman army with control over 100 soldiers. Roman soldiers, of all people, were hated by the Jews for their oppression, power, control, and ridicule. Yet this man's genuine faith amazed Jesus! This hated Gentile's faith put to shame the stagnant piety of many of the Jewish religious leaders.

Jesus told the crowd that many religious Jews who should be in the Kingdom would be excluded because of their lack of faith. Entrenched in their religious traditions, they could not accept Christ and His new message. We must be careful not to become so set in our religious habits that we expect God to work only in specified ways. Don't limit God by your mindset and lack of faith.

'The East and the West' described in Matthew 8:11 stands for the four corners of the earth. All the faithful people of God will be gathered to the feast with the Messiah (see Isaiah 6 & Isaiah 55). The Jews should have known when the Messiah came; His blessings would be for the Gentiles also, (see Isaiah 66:12 & 19). But this message came as a shock because they were too wrapped up in their own affairs and destiny. In claiming God's promises, we must not apply them so personally that we forget to see what God wants to do to reach all the people He loves.

Luke 7:2 (KJV); "There a centurion's servant, whom his master valued highly, was sick and about to die."

Luke 7:3 (KJV); "And when he heard of Jesus, he sent unto him the elders of the Jews, beseeching him that he would come and heal his servant."

Why did the centurion send Jewish elders to Jesus instead of going himself? Since he was well aware of the Jewish hatred for Roman soldiers, he may not have wanted to interrupt a Jewish gathering. As an army captain, he daily delegated work and sent groups on missions, so this was how he chose to get his message to Jesus.

Matthew 8:5 says the Roman centurion visited Jesus Himself, while Luke 7:3 says he sent Jewish elders to present his request to Jesus. In dealing with the messengers, Jesus was dealing with the centurion. For his Jewish audience, Matthew emphasized the man's faith. For his Gentile audience, Luke highlighted the good relationship between the Jewish elders and the Roman centurion.

Luke 7:4 (NIV); "When they came to Jesus, they pleaded earnestly with him, 'This man deserves to have you do this.'"

Luke 7:5 (NIV); "'Because he loves our nation and has built our synagogue.'"

Luke 7:6 (NIV); "So Jesus went with them. He was not far from the house when the centurion sent friends to say to him: 'Lord, don't trouble yourself, for I do not deserve to have you come under my roof.'"

Luke 7:7 (NIV); "'That is why I did not even consider myself worthy to come to you. But say the word, and my servant will be healed.'"

Luke 7:8 (NIV); "For I myself am a man under authority, with soldiers under me. I tell this one, 'Go,' and he goes; and that one, 'Come,' and he comes. I say to my servant, 'Do this,' and he does it."

The Roman centurion didn't come to Jesus, and he didn't expect Jesus to come to him. This officer did not need to be present to have his orders carried out, so Jesus didn't need to be present to heal. The centurion's faith was especially surprising because he was a Gentile who had not been brought up to know a loving God.

Luke 7:9 (NIV); "When Jesus heard this, he was amazed at him, and turning to the crowd following him, he said, 'I tell you, I have not found such faith even in Israel.'"

Luke 7:10 (NIV); "Then the men who had been sent returned to the house and found the servant well."

Healing requires faith today just as it did two thousand years ago.

Matthew 8:14 (NIV); "When Jesus came into Peter's house, he saw Peter's mother-in-law lying in bed with a fever."

Matthew 8:15 (NIV); "He touched her hand and the fever left her, and she got up and began to wait on him."

Peter's mother-in-law gives us a beautiful example to follow. Her response to Jesus' touch was to wait-on Jesus and his disciples–immediately. Has God ever helped you through a dangerous or difficult situation? If so, you should ask, "How can I express my gratitude to Him?" Because God has promised us all the rewards of His kingdom, we should look for ways to serve Him and His followers now.

Mark 1:30 (NIV); "Simon's mother-in-law was in bed with a fever, and they immediately told Jesus about her."

Mark 1:31 (NIV); "So he went to her, took her hand and helped her up. The fever left her and she began to wait on them."

Each Gospel writer had a slightly different perspective as he wrote; thus the comparable stories in the Gospels often highlight different details. In Matthew, Jesus touched the woman's hand. In Mark, He helped her up. In Luke, Jesus spoke to the fever, and it left her. The accounts do not conflict. Each writer chose to emphasize different details of the story in order to highlight a certain characteristic of Jesus.

Luke 4:38 (NIV); "Jesus left the synagogue and went to the home of Simon. Now Simon's mother-in-law was suffering from a high fever, and they asked Jesus to help her."

Luke 4:39 (NIV); "So he bent over her and rebuked the fever, and it left her. She got up at once and began to wait on them."

Again we see Jesus healing someone by laying hands on the person. Notice that she was up and was healed. This is an important principle we will see over and over in these Scripture passages. It is essential for the sick person to put his or her faith into action. Many times the healings don't happen until people mix action with their faith. This is just as true today as it was in the first century.

Also, notice Jesus did not pray for the woman to be healed. He told the fever to go, and He rebuked it, and it left her. Healing often works precisely the same way today.

Matthew 8:16 (NIV); "When evening came, many who were demon-possessed were brought to him, and he spoke to the spirits with a word and healed the sick."

Matthew 8:17 (NIV); "This was to fulfill what was spoken through the prophet Isaiah: 'He took up our infirmities and bore [carried] our diseases.'"

How could the disciples experience so many of Jesus' miracles and yet be so slow to comprehend who He was? They had already seen Jesus feed over 5,000 people with five loaves and two fish (Mark 6:35-44), yet here they doubted whether He could feed another large group.

Sometimes we are also slow to learn. Although Christ has brought us through trials and temptations in the past, we don't believe that He will do it in the future. Is your heart too closed to take in all that God can do for you? Don't be like the disciples. Remember what Christ has done, and have faith He will do it again.

'Notes'

⇦⇦⇦   Blank page added for 'Notes.'

Blank page added for 'Notes.'

CHAPTER 17

BECAUSE OF YOUR UNBELIEF

Written by Dr. Harold Bollinger

Matthew 17:19-20 (KJV); "[19-]Then came the disciples to Jesus apart, and said, Why could not we cast him out? [20-]And Jesus said unto them, Because of your unbelief: for verily I say unto you, If ye have faith as a grain of mustard seed, ye shall say unto this mountain, Remove hence to yonder place; and it shall remove; and nothing shall be impossible to you."

When the Lord Jesus sent His disciples into different parts of Palestine, He endued them with double power, that of casting out unclean spirits and that of healing all sickness and all infirmity (Matthew 10:1). He did the same for the seventy who came back to Him with joy, saying, "...Lord, even the demons submit to us in your name."—Luke 10:17 (NIV). On the day of the Transfiguration, while the Lord was still upon the mountain, a father brought his son who was possessed with a demon, to His disciples, imploring them to cast out the evil spirit, but they could not. When, after Jesus had cured the child, the disciples asked Him why they had been unable to do it themselves as in other cases, He answered them, "...Because of your unbelief...."—Matthew 17:20 (KJV). It was, then, their unbelief, and

not the Will of God which had been the cause of their defeat.

Today, divine healing is believed-in very little because it has almost entirely disappeared from the Christian Church. One may ask for the reason, and here are the two answers which have been given. The greater numbers of believers think that miracles, the gift of healing included, should be limited to the time of the primitive Church, that their object was to establish the first foundation of Christianity, but that from that time circumstances have altered. Other believers say that if the Church has lost these gifts, it is her own fault; it is because she has become worldly that the Spirit acts but feebly in her; it is because she has not remained in direct and habitual relation with the full power of the unseen world; but that if she were to see anew springing up within her men and women who live the life of faith and of the Holy Spirit, entirely consecrated to their God, she would see the manifestation of the same gifts as in former times again. Which of these two opinions coincide the most with the Word of God? Is it by the Will of God that the "Gifts of Healing" (1 Corinthians 12:9) have been suppressed, or is it rather man who is responsible for it? Is it the Will of God that miracles should not take place?

Will He in consequence of this no longer give the faith which produces them? Or again, is it the Church which has been guilty of lacking faith?

What Do the Scriptures Say?

The Bible does not authorize us, either by the words of the Lord or His apostles, to believe that the gifts of healing were granted only to the early times of the Church. On the contrary, the promises which Jesus made to the apostles when He gave them instructions concerning their mission, shortly before His ascension, appear to us applicable to all times.

Mark 16:15-18 (KJV)

15. "And he said unto them, Go ye into all the world, and preach the gospel to every creature.

16. He that believeth and is baptized shall be saved; but he that believeth not shall be damned.

17. And these signs shall follow them that believe; In my name shall they cast out devils; they shall speak with new tongues;

18. They shall take up serpents; and if they drink any deadly thing, it shall not hurt them; they shall lay hands on the sick, and they shall recover."

Paul places the gift of healing among the operations of the Holy Spirit.

1 Corinthians 12:9 (KJV); "To another faith by the same Spirit; to another the gifts of healing by the same Spirit."

James gives a precise command on this matter without any restriction of time.

James 5:13-16 (KJV)

13. "Is any among you afflicted? Let him pray. Is any merry? Let him sing psalms.

14. Is any sick among you? Let him call for the elders of the church; and let them pray over him, anointing him with oil in the Name of the Lord:

15. And the prayer of faith shall save the sick, and the Lord shall raise him up; and if he has committed sins, they shall be forgiven him.

16. Confess your faults one to another, and pray one for another, that ye may be healed. The effectual fervent prayer of a righteous man availeth much."

The entire Scriptures declare that these graces will be granted according to the measure of the Spirit and of faith.

It is also alleged that at the outset of each new dispensation God works miracles, that it is His ordinary course of action; but it is nothing of the kind. Think of the people of God in the former dispensation, in the time of Abraham, all through the life of Moses, in the exodus from Egypt, under Joshua, in the time of the Judges and of Samuel, under the reign of David and other godly kings up to Daniel's time; during more than a thousand years miracles took place.

But, it is said, miracles were much more necessary in the early days of Christianity than later. But what about the power of heathenism even in this day, wherever the Gospel seeks to combat it? It is impossible to admit that miracles should have been more needful for the

heathen in Ephesus (Acts 19:11-12) than for the heathen of Africa in the present day.

Acts 19:11-12 (KJV)
11. "And God wrought special miracles by the hands of Paul:
12. So that from his body were brought unto the sick handkerchiefs or aprons, and the diseases departed from them, and the evil spirits went out of them."

And if we think of the ignorance and unbelief which reign even in the midst of the Christian nations, are we not driven to conclude that there is a need for manifest acts of the power of God to sustain the testimony of believers and to prove that God is with them? Besides, among believers themselves, how much of doubt, how much of weakness there is! How their faith needs to be awakened and stimulated by some evident proof of the presence of the Lord in their midst. One part of our being consists of flesh and blood; it is therefore in flesh and blood that God Wills to manifest His presence.

In order to prove that it is the Church's unbelief which has lost the gift of healing, let us see what the Bible says about it. Does it not often put us on our guard against unbelief, against all which can estrange and turn us from our God? Does not the history of the Church show us the necessity of these warnings? Does it not furnish us with numerous examples of backward steps, of world pleasing, in which faith grew weak in the exact measure in which the spirit of the world took

the upper hand? Such faith is only possible to Him who lives in the invisible world.

2 Corinthians 5:7 (KJV); "(For we walk by faith, not by sight.)"

Until the third century the healings by faith in Christ were numerous, but in the centuries following, they became more infrequent. Do we not know from the Bible that it is always unbelief which hinders the mighty working of God?

Oh, that we could learn to believe in the promises of God! God has not gone back from His promises; Jesus is still He who heals both soul and body; salvation offers us even now healing, holiness, and the Holy Spirit is always ready to give us some manifestations of his power. Even when we ask why this divine power is not more often seen, He answers us: "Because of your unbelief." The more we give ourselves to experience personally sanctification by faith, the more we shall also experience healing by faith. These two doctrines walk abreast. The more the Spirit of God lives and acts in the soul of believers, the more will the miracles multiply by which He works in the body. Thereby the world can recognize what redemption means.

'Notes'

⇦⇦⇦　　　Blank page added for 'Notes.'

Blank page added for 'Notes.' ⇨⇨⇨

CHAPTER 18

POWER GIVEN TO BELIEVERS

Jesus has given believers all power and authority in His name. It is a great challenge to accept and act upon His Words as given.

God's 'Love' Destroyed the Works of Satin

John 3:16 (NKJV); "...God so loved the world that he gave his only begotten son." How wonderful it is to know that God loved us so much that He paid a high price for our freedom or redemption. He gave His Son as our substitute, who assumed our guilt, bore our judgment and endured our condemnation in order to absolve us of all debt and obligation to Satan's regime so that we could be restored to God as though no sin had ever been committed. He legally redeemed us. God proved how much you are valued–and wants us to be able to share his best with us, his abundant life.

God is love; salvation is your freedom from everything outside of God's Will for mankind. Now you can act accordingly. You may speak the language of a winner. God so loved us that He gave His Son as our substitute.

Confess your freedom, instead of your bondage. Confess: with his stripes, I am healed, instead of your sicknesses. Confess your redemption from all disease. Confess that your redemption is complete, from sin and from sickness.

Confess that Satan's dominion over you ended at Calvary because it was there that God freed you. God's Word states all of this, so confess it.

Tell Satan you found the truth, the truth that sets you free from him. Let him know by your confession of God's Word, that you are free from his domain and that you know it.

The statement, He, Jesus, has borne our grief (sicknesses) and carried our sorrows (diseases) is God's promise of perfect healing. Confess it, and perfect health will be manifest in your body.

The sicknesses and diseases of your body were laid on Jesus. You need never bear them because He has borne them for you. All you need to do is believe this and begin to confess it.

Galatians 2:20 (KJV); "I am crucified with Christ: nevertheless I live; yet not I, but Christ liveth in me: and the life which I now live in the flesh I live by the faith of the Son of God, who loved me, and gave himself for me."

When Jesus was crucified, I was crucified with Him. When they buried Jesus, I was buried with Him. When Jesus arose from the grave as a conqueror, I arose with Him as a conqueror. See Colossians 3:1 & Romans 6:4-5. He has quickened us (made us alive) together with Christ and has raised us up together with Christ.

Satan, the sickness you tried to put on me was destroyed on the cross of Calvary, for me, and I do not have to bear it. I command you, in Jesus name, leave my body. I'm free from your curse, for it is written: with his stripes, I am healed, so I am healed. Jesus said so, Satan, you are a liar, your pains are lies, your symptoms are lies, and your words are lies. You are the father of lies, Jesus said you are (see John 8:44).

Then begin to praise God for your deliverance. You are set free, and Satan is a defeated foe. Don't allow him to intimidate you or to make you believe that he has any control over you because he does not. Only you can allow him to control your life, put a stop to it now, just say in Jesus name Satan get behind me and he has to go.

When Jesus went back to the throne and sat on the right hand of God, He made us sit together with him in heavenly places. We are God's workmanship, created in Christ Jesus our Lord. Through Jesus Christ, God made us what we are, and that is a new creation. 2 Corinthians 5:17 (KJV); "Therefore if anyone be in Christ, he is a new creature *[creation]:* old things are passed away, behold, all things are become new."

In Romans 8:37 (KJV) Paul says, "…in all these things we are more than conquerors through him that loved us." We are now new creations, made in the image and likeness of God through the power of Jesus Christ; God gives us His nature, His love, His faith, His life, His spirit, and His power. We are re-created, made new.

All that Jesus did was for us. Everything He conquered was for us. Jesus had no need to conquer Satan for Himself. He had no sin of His own because He had no sin until He took our sins. Jesus did all of this for us.

Jesus had no need to put away sickness for Himself because He had no sickness until He was made sick with our sickness. He did this for us. He conquered for us; and now that we are re-created in Christ Jesus and are made partakers with Him, we become conquerors also through Him. Remember in all these things, we are more than conquerors, through Jesus Christ that loved us.

Jesus' death, burial, and resurrection were for us. All that Jesus did was for us, and we are now partakers of His victory. We were prisoners, but Jesus has set us free from that prison. We were cursed by sin and sickness; but Jesus, our Redeemer, has freed us from the curse and loosed us from its domain.

We were weak, but the Lord has put our weakness away, and He has become our strength, so now we are

strong. We were bound and imprisoned, but Christ has freed us from slavery. We were sick, but Christ has borne our sicknesses and carried them away, so now, with His stripes, we are healed.

We don't have to be a slave any longer. We are free. Shout your freedom to the world. Confess your freedom. Believe in your freedom. Redemption is a fact. Act on your liberty. Your bondage has passed. Your prison is open. Your freedom is hereby granted.

Isaiah 61:1 (KJV); "The Spirit of the Lord God is upon me; because the Lord has anointed me to preach good tidings unto the meek; he hath sent me to bind up the brokenhearted, to proclaim liberty to the captives, and the opening of the prison to them that are bound."

Satan can never harm you unless you let him. Always remember Psalm 34:7 (KJV); "The angel of the Lord encampeth round about them that fear *[reverence]* him, and delivereth them." You never need to be fearful in the presence of God's Angels and of the Lord Himself at your home. Jesus said, "...I will never leave thee, nor forsake thee."—Hebrews 13:5 (KJV). He's always there.

If disease or sickness is threatening you, do not confess it. Confess God's Word: "...with his stripes, I am healed" (see Isaiah 53:5). You must say what God says, confessing His Word. Disease gains the upper hand when you agree with the testimony of your natural

senses. Your five senses have no place in the round of faith.

Confessing disease, sickness, pain, and problems is like signing for a package at the post office. Satan then has received your confession from you showing that you have accepted his package.

Do not accept anything sent by Satan. Even though your five senses might testify that it has come to you, refuse to confess it. Look for the promise in the Word that gives you victory. Always remember you were healed, it is a finished work, and it belongs to you.

Sickness comes from the devil. When you tell others of your troubles and sicknesses, you're giving testimony to Satan's ability to get you into trouble in sickness. When you talk about your sickness and disease, you're glorifying the adversary who had the ability to put their disease or sickness on you.

People like sympathy and pity. These can never help your pain. Sympathy can never get you well. Sympathy is us suffering with another person. What you need is not sympathy, but a substitution, which is suffering for another. Jesus did not come to be your sympathizer. He became your substitute, which is suffering for another.

We as Christians often pray for the sick, our position as believers is not to sympathize with the sick and pity them because of their pain but to assume authority over

disease on the basis of Christ's substitution, and we command pains and sicknesses to leave in Jesus name.

Let me finish this chapter with Joshua 1:9 (KJV), God said unto Joshua, "...Be strong and of good courage; be not afraid, neither be thou dismayed: for the Lord thy *[your]* God is with thee...." Then He said, "There shall not any person be able to stand before you all the days of your life...."—Joshua 1:5 (KJV). And Jesus says to you, "Behold, I give unto you power to tread on serpents and scorpions, and over all the power of the enemy: and nothing shall by any means hurt you." That's in Luke 10:19.

'Notes'

Blank page added for 'Notes.'

CHAPTER 19

WHAT YOU SAY IS WHAT YOU GET

Mark 11:22-23 (KJV); "²² And Jesus answering saith unto them, Have faith in God. ²³ For verily I say unto you, That whosoever shall say unto this mountain, Be thou removed, and be thou cast into the sea; and shall not doubt in his heart, but shall believe that those things which he saith shall come to pass; he shall have whatsoever he saith."

Proverbs 4:20-22 (KJV); "²⁰ My son, attend to my words; incline thine ear unto my sayings. ²¹ Let them not depart from thine eyes; keep them in the midst of thine heart. ²² For they *[God's Words]* are life unto those that find them, and health to all their flesh."

Don't talk about your problems, talk about what God said about the situation.

When sickness shows up, don't talk about it, quote Psalm 103 (I forgive all of your sins, and I heal all of your sicknesses). Never talk the problem.

God answered and said, "My son, just as I was with Jesus, so will I be with you. You go and cast out devils. You heal the sick. You cleanse the lepers. You raise the dead. I give you power over all the power of the

enemy. Do not be afraid. Be strong. Be courageous. I am with you as I was with Jesus. No demon should be able to stand before you all the days of your life. I used men and women then, but now I desire to use you."

God's River of Blessings

Romans 5:17 (KJV); "For if by one man's offense [Adam] death reigned by one; much more they which receive abundance of grace and of the gift of righteousness shall reign in life by one Jesus Christ."

Romans 8:28 (KJV); "And we know that all things work together for good to them that love God, to them who are the called according to his purpose."

Romans 8:32 (KJV); "He that spared not his own Son, but delivered him up for us all, how shall he not with him also freely give us all things."

1 Corinthians 3:21 (NKJV); "Therefore let no one boast in men. For all things are yours."

3 John 1:2 (KJV); "Beloved, I wish above all things that thou mayest prosper and be in health, even as thy soul prospereth."

Proverbs 10:22 (KJV); "The blessing of the Lord, it maketh rich, and he addeth no sorrow with it."

Proverbs 10:24 (KJV); "The fear of the wicked, it shall come upon him: but the desire of the righteous shall be granted."

We all desire to be in the flow of God's blessings, and God makes it clear what is required, we must begin to observe and do God's Word.

Matthew 7:26-27 (KJV); "[26]And every one that heareth these sayings *[words]* of mine, and doeth them not, shall be likened unto a foolish man, who built his house upon the sand; [27]and the rains descended, and the floods came, and the winds blew, and beat upon that house: and it fell: and great was the fall of it."

Everyone who hears these sayings and acts on them will be found to resemble a wise man who built his house upon the rock. The rock is doing the Word. He that does <u>not</u> do, the Word never builds up a solid foundation.

And every one that heareth these words and doeth them not shall be likened to a foolish man who built his house upon the sand. The hearer must become a doer or else the entire structure that he builds will be destroyed, Jesus illustrated that. Jesus made us know what acting on the word really means.

The wise man is a doer of the Word. The other hears but does not act upon it. He is a sense knowledge hearer. He hears the Word, but he is not a doer. He responds to reason instead of the Word. His spiritual

life is built on sand. You can tell whether a man is building on the sand or on the rock, by noticing whether he is practicing the Word or not, whether he is acting on the Word.

James 1:22-25 (NKJV); "[22]But be doers of the word, and not hearers only, deceiving yourselves, [23]For if anyone is a hearer of the word and not a doer, he is like a man observing his natural face in a mirror; [24]for he observes himself, goes away, and immediately forgets what kind of man he was. [25]But he that looks into the perfect law of liberty and continues *in it*, and is not a forgetful hearer but a doer of the work, this one *[man]* will be blessed in what he does."

It is the doer of the Word, the man who practices it, lives it, walks in it, that builds it into his own life, whom God honors.

The Law of Love

God is love and they that love are born of God and knows God (see 1 John 4:7-8 below).

The new birth which makes a man a new creation is the receiving of this love-nature from God by mankind.

1 John 4:7-8 (KJV); "[7]Beloved, let us love one another: for love is of God; and every one that loveth is born of God, and knoweth God. [8]He that loveth not knoweth not God for God is love."

The love test shows the world that either you're one of God's children or that you're not one of God's children. 1 John 3:14 (KJV); "We know that we have passed from death unto life, because we love the brethren. He that loveth not his brother abideth in death." If your life shows forth the love of God, the Word says you have been begotten of God and know God. And that if a man does not love, regardless of his religious profession, he is abiding in spiritual death, alienated from God.

The Greek word for 'love' used here, makes it easy to understand this God kind of love, the word for love used here is 'Agape.' It seems that Jesus coined this word when He expressed the new love law that was to govern the new creation in the following words: "[34]A new commandment I give unto you, that you love one another; as I have loved you, that you also love one another. [35]By this all will know that you are My disciples if you have love one to another."—John 13:34-35 (NKJV).

Man received a new nature which brings him into a new family, the family of God and makes him a new creation with a new Father and they are to be a new people. This new love would make known to the world that they had become children of the God of love, for they receive the love nature of their Heavenly Father.

We can see this love in Romans 5:5 (KJV); "…The love of God is shed abroad in our hearts by the Holy Ghost…." What is this that is shed abroad? It is the

love of God. It is the manifestation of the nature of God within us. When one is born from above, the Father's nature comes into his spirit. That nature manifests itself in love. His divine love, which is radically different from our old human love, although it operates through the same facilities. When Jesus was here the Greek word used was 'phileo,' which means human love, as the love of a mother for her child, or the love of her husband for his wife. At that time that was the highest type of love, that man had ever known.

There was no other word for a higher type of love then phileo. This common human love of ours is the most blessed asset of the human, and yet the most dangerous. This phileo love is the goddess of the divorce court. It is the high priests of human suffering, the parent of most of our tears, sorrow, and heartache. It turns to jealousy and murder at the slightest provocation. It is pure selfishness; it feeds only on self-gratification.

But Jesus brings a new kind of love, a love that seeketh not its own. Agape love. This kind of love is the real heart cry of God. This old kind of love is from the natural human heart: this new kind of love springs forth from the re-created born again spirit of man and the very heart of God. One is the manifestation of God in the new man; the other is natural man. Self or selfishness is the very center of phileo love. Agape love is God at work in the new creation born again spirit man and God demonstrates this love through His children. This agape love is not only the law of the family of

God, but it is also the life and joy of the human family. It makes Christianity more beautiful than all the other religions of the Earth. It makes the life of the Saints the sweetest life and the most fragrant of all human races.

The prayer of Christianity must be, 'Father, forgive them for they know not what they do.' This is Agape love in action. It breathes the fragrance of forgiveness. It speaks forth in humility. It is a strength clothed in gentleness. It makes the strong bear the burdens of the weak, the rich pay the bills of the poor; it is the love of Christ manifested among natural man. 1 Corinthians 13 shows us this Agape love in action. It comes directly from the throne of God. It is God's own description of His life and nature at work through natural man.

1 Corinthians 13:1-13 (KJV)
1. "Though I speak with the tongues of men and of angels, and have not love, I am become as sounding brass, or a tinkling cymbal.
2. And though I have the gift of prophecy, and understand all mysteries, and all knowledge; and though I have all faith, so that I could remove mountains, and have not love, I am nothing.
3. And though I bestow all my goods to feed the poor, and though I give my body to be burned, and have not love, it profiteth me nothing.
4. Love suffereth long *and* is kind; love envieth not; love vaunteth not itself, is not puffed up.
5. Doth not behave itself unseemly, seeketh not her own, is not easily provoked, thinketh no evil;
6. Rejoiceth not in iniquity, but rejoiceth in the truth;

7. Beareth all things, believeth all things, hopeth all things, endureth all things.

8. Love never faileth: but whether there be prophecies, they shall fail; whether there be tongues, they shall cease; whether there be knowledge, it shall vanish away.

9. for we know in part, and we prophesy in part.

10. But when that which is perfect is come, then that which is in part shall be done away.

11. When I was a child, I spake as a child, I understood as a child, I thought as a child: but when I became a man, I put away childish things.

12. For now we see through a glass, darkly; but then face to face: now I know in part; but then shall I know even as also I am known.

13. And now abideth faith, hope, love, these three; but the greatest of these is love."

This Agape love is God's one key ingredient in His program for mankind; it satisfies all of God's required.

Agape love cannot fail, therefore never fails, and it satisfies all of the requirements of God, for the Scripture says it this way "love [Agape] is the fulfilling of the law," this love should be our highest aim in this life!

Ministering Angels

Psalm 91:11 (NKJV); "For He shall give His angels charge over you, To keep you in all your ways."

Hebrews 13:1-2 (NKJV); "[1]Let brotherly love continue. [2]Do not forget to entertain strangers, for by so *doing* some have unwittingly entertained angels."

The Magic of Love

Love is like magic and always will be for love still remains life's sweet mystery! Love works in ways that are wondrous and strange. There is nothing in life that love cannot change! Love cannot be bought for it is priceless and free. Love is like pure magic; a sweet mystery!

2 Peter 1:2-4 (NKJV)
2. "Grace and peace be multiplied to you in the knowledge of God and of Jesus our Lord,
3. As His divine power has given to us all things that *pertain* unto life and godliness, through the knowledge of him who called us by glory and virtue,
4. By which have been given to us exceeding great and precious promises, that through these you may be partakers of the divine nature, having escaped the corruption *that is* in the world through lust."

What You Say is What You Get

Let's get back to, 'What you say.' Are you aware that Isaiah 57:19 says that "I *[God]* create*[s]* the fruit of your lips…" or what you say?

Isaiah 57:19 (KJV); "I create the fruit of the lips; Peace, peace to him that is far off, and to him that is near, saith the LORD; and I will heal him."

Your Confession Rules You

Confession brings possession. Nothing is any more important in our walk as a believer than our confession. Christianity is called the great confession, in Hebrews 3.

The Greek word for 'confession' is translated 'profession.' In other words, it means to say what God says in His Word. In other words, we are to speak God's words back to Him.

You Reap What You Speak

Joshua 1:8 (KJV); "This book of the law shall not depart out of thy mouth; but thou shalt meditate therein day and night, that thou mayest observe to do according to all that is written therein: for then thou shalt make thy way prosperous, and then thou shalt have good success."

If you want success, you must speak God's Word back to Him. The Greek word for *confession* actually means "to say the same thing" and then "Agree, Admit, acknowledge." We are to say what God has said in His Word about us. When you believe in your heart and confess with your mouth, your prayers will be answered.

By Christ's stripes, I am healed. He heals all my sicknesses. Christ Himself took my infirmities and bore my sickness. Let's talk the language of God's Word at all times.

No weapon formed against me can prosper. All things work together for my good. Remember God creates the fruit of thy lips.

WHAT YOU SAY IS WHAT YOU GET!

'Notes'

Blank page added for 'Notes.'

CHAPTER 20

SCRIPTURAL HEALING

Divine healing is the POWER OF GOD to heal the sick in answer to believing prayer.

It is a GIFT of God to those who believe, just as salvation or the baptism with the Holy Spirit is a GIFT to those who believe.

Isaiah 53:1-12 (KJV)
1. "Who hath believed our report? and to whom is the arm of the Lord revealed?
2. For he shall grow up before him as a tender plant, and as a root out of a dry ground: he hath no form nor comeliness; and when we shall see him, there is no beauty that we should desire him.
3. He is despised and rejected of men; a man of sorrows, and acquainted with grief: and we hid as it were our faces from him; he was despised, and we esteemed him not.
4. Surely he hath borne our griefs, and carried our sorrows: yet we did esteem him stricken, smitten of God, and afflicted.
5. But he was wounded for our transgressions, he was bruised for our iniquities: the chastisement of our peace was upon him; and with his stripes we are healed.

6. All we like sheep have gone astray; we have turned every one to his own way; and the Lord hath laid on him the iniquity of us all.

7. He was oppressed, and he was afflicted, yet he opened not his mouth: he is brought as a lamb to the slaughter, and as a sheep before her shearers is dumb, so he openeth not his mouth.

8. He was taken from prison and from judgment: and who shall declare his generation? for he was cut off out of the land of the living: for the transgression of my people was he stricken.

9. And he made his grave with the wicked, and with the rich in his death; because he had done no violence, neither was any deceit in his mouth.

10. Yet it pleased the Lord to bruise him; he hath put him to grief: when thou shalt make his soul an offering for sin, he shall see his seed, he shall prolong his days, and the pleasure of the Lord shall prosper in his hand.

11. He shall see of the travail of his soul, and shall be satisfied: by his knowledge shall my righteous servant justify many; for he shall bear their iniquities.

12. Therefore will I divide him a portion with the great, and he shall divide the spoil with the strong; because he hath poured out his soul unto death: and he was numbered with the transgressors; and he bare the sin of many, and made intercession for the transgressors."

We DO NOT receive healing because we are good or deserve it. We receive healing because Jesus Christ

paid for it at the whipping post, and it is ours for the asking if we believe.

1 Peter 2:24 (KJV); "Who his own self bare our sins in his own body on the tree, that we, being dead to sins, should live unto righteousness: by whose stripes ye were healed."

It says in Isaiah 53:5 that Christ has bore our griefs, carried our sorrows, was wounded for our transgressions, was bruised for our iniquities, and with His stripes, we are healed. Jesus paid the total price for the total deliverance, for the total person.

Work Out Your Own Salvation

Scripture indicates that the soul is in need of healing when we fail to keep the commandments of God.

3 John 1:2 (KJV); "Beloved, I wish above all things that thou mayest prosper and be in health, even as thy soul prospereth."

Some of the things that cause sickness…

1. Intemperance, Proverbs 25:16 and Psalm 127:2.
2. Sin, John 5:5-14.
3. Disobedience and murmuring, Exodus 15:22-26.
4. Speaking against God's anointed, Numbers 12:1-15.
5. Satan, Job 1 and Job 2:7.

Believing Prayer

"The effectual fervent prayer of the righteous man availeth much."—James 5:16 (KJV).

FAITH has always been the prerequisite for divine healing. Look at the many times Jesus healed while He was here on earth.

1. The paralytic healed (Luke 5:17-20). Who had faith?
2. The centurion's servant healed (Luke 7:1-10). Who had faith?
3. The woman bowed together for 18 years (Luke 13:10-13). Who had faith?

Other Methods

James 5:13 (KJV); "Is any sick among you? Let him call for the elders of the church; and LET THEM PRAY over him, anointing him with oil in the name of the Lord."

James 5:16 (KJV); "Confess your faults one to another, and PRAY ONE FOR ANOTHER, that ye may be healed…."

Pulling Down Strongholds

Basically, all illness comes from Satan. He is the one who has come "…to steal, and to kill, and to destroy."—John 10:10 (NKJV).

"And I *[Jesus]* will give you *[followers]* the keys of the kingdom of heaven; and whatsoever you *[shall]* bind on earth will be bound in heaven, and whatsoever you loose on earth shall be loosed in heaven."—Matthew 16:19 (NKJV).

"Cast down imaginations, and every high thing that exalteth itself against the knowledge of God, and bringing into captivity every thought to the obedience of Christ."—2 Corinthians 10:5 (KJV).

The Great Commission

MARK 16:15 & 17 (KJV)

15. "GO YE INTO ALL THE WORLD AND PREACH THE GOSPEL TO EVERY CREATURE.

17. AND THESE SIGNS SHALL FOLLOW...."

'Notes'

Blank page added for 'Notes.'

CHAPTER 21

JESUS HEALED ALL WHO CAME TO HIM

It was a sign of God's love and compassion as well as a sign which drew people to repentance, and recognition of Jesus Christ as the Messiah. Miracles continue today for the same purposes. These lessons will acquaint the student with knowledge of how to move in the miraculous.

The Word of God is the Life of God. Believe it, receive it and act upon it!

Jesus has become the guarantee of a better covenant; Hebrews 7:22 (NKJV); "Therefore He is also able to save to the uttermost those who come to God through Him, since He always lives to make intercession for them."

Take a look at this Scripture, Hebrews 7:22 in the Amplified Bible, Classic Edition (AMPC): "Therefore He is able also to save to the uttermost (completely, perfectly, finally, and for all time and eternity) those who come to God through Him, since He is always living to make petition to God and intercede with Him and intervene for them."

This "better covenant" is also called the new covenant or testament. It is new and better because it allows us to go directly to God through Christ. We no longer need to rely on sacrificed animals and mediating priests to obtain God's forgiveness. This new covenant is better because, while all human priests die, Christ lives forever. Priests and sacrifices could not save people, but Christ truly saves. You have access to Christ. He is available to you.

No one can add to what Jesus did to save us; our past, present, and future sins are all forgiven, and Jesus is with the Father as a sign that our sins are forgiven. If you are a Christian, remember that Christ has paid the price for your sins once and for all (see also Hebrews 9:24-28).

As our high priest, Christ is our advocate, the mediator between God and us. He looks after our interests and intercedes for us with God. The Old Testament high priest went before God once a year to plead for the forgiveness of the nation's sins; Christ makes perpetual intercession before God for us. Christ's continuous presence in heaven with the Father assures us that our sins have been paid for and forgiven (see Romans 8:33-34; Hebrews 2:17-18; Hebrews 4:15-16; & Hebrews 9:24). This wonderful assurance frees us from guilt and from fear of failure.

It is important to remember the word 'Save' is the Greek word 'SOZO,' which literally means to heal, preserve, save, do well, and be (make) whole. It means

deliverance in the present as well as in the future or in eternity, physical as well as spiritual. Jesus used this word to denote healing of the body as well as forgiveness of sins. Always translate this word as "save-heal" when you come across it in the word.

In Acts 5:16, the Bible says the crowds came in from the villages around Jerusalem, bringing their sick, and those possessed by evil spirits. They were all healed.

What did these miraculous healings do for the early church?

1. They attracted new believers.
2. They confirmed the truth of the apostles teaching.
3. They demonstrated the power of the Messiah, who had been crucified and risen, was now with his followers.

Even after Jesus had been crucified and rose again, and ascended into heaven, we see the very same work Jesus performed still taking place through the hands of His disciples with the very same intensity - all being healed. And why not? Hebrews 13:8 tells us Jesus Christ is the same yesterday, today, and forever!

The religious leaders were jealous–Peter and the apostles were already commanding more respect than the religious leaders had ever received. The difference, however, was the religious leaders demanded respect and reverence for themselves; the Apostles' goal was to bring respect and reverence to God. The Apostles were

respected not because they demanded it, but because they deserved it.

The Apostles experienced the power to do miracles, great boldness in preaching, and God's presence in their lives. Yet they were not free from hatred and persecution. They were arrested, put in jail, beaten, and slandered by community leaders. Faith in God does not make troubles disappear; it makes troubles appear less frightening because it puts them in the right perspective. Don't expect everyone to react favorably when you share something as dynamic as your faith in Christ. Some will be jealous, afraid, or threatened. Expect some negative reactions, and remember you must be more concerned about serving God than about the reactions of people (see Acts 5:29).

Acts 13:38-39 (NKJV); "[38-]Therefore let it be known to you, brethren, that through this Man *[Jesus]* is preached to you the forgiveness of sins; [39-]and by Him everyone who believes is justified *[declared righteous]* from all things from which you could not be justified by the Law of Moses."

Train yourself to translate the word 'justified' as declared righteous. Justified is the literal Greek translation. This will really help when you read the book of Romans. You can remember it by 'just-if-I'd' never sinned.

That is righteousness–to be in right standing with God. 2 Corinthians 5:21 tells us plainly that as born-

again believers we have become the righteousness of God in Christ. Because of the forgiveness of sins, through His shed blood, we are redeemed and declared righteous from ALL THINGS which we could not be declared righteous, apart from His redemptive work. This is our position in Christ, and it's more than just spiritual, the effects of it pertain to the soul, the body and our life here on this earth.

Romans 8:11 (NKJV); "But if the Spirit of Him who raised Jesus from the dead dwells in you, He who raised Christ from the dead will also give life to your mortal *[Natural, Earthly]* bodies through His Spirit who dwells in you."

Take a close look at this Scripture; this is talking about your body you now have, not the one you're going to receive one day in heaven! Allow the Lord to impart His life into you by placing faith in His Word. Begin to praise Him for this promise.

2 Corinthians 4:10-11 (KJV); "[10]"Always bearing about in the body the dying of the Lord Jesus, that the life also of Jesus might be made manifest in our body. [11]"For we which live are always delivered unto death for Jesus' sake, that the life also of Jesus might be made manifest in our mortal flesh." Bodily Health!

Paul reminds us that though we may think we are at the end of the rope, we are never at the end of hope. Our perishable bodies are subject to sin and suffering, but God never abandons us. Because Christ has won

the victory over death, we have eternal life. All our risks, humiliations, and trials are opportunities for Christ to demonstrate his power and presence in and through us.

Matthew 6:9-10 (KJV); "[9]...Our Father which art in heaven, Hallowed be thy name. [10]Thy kingdom comes, Thy will be done in *[on]* earth, as it is in heaven."

Jesus always prays the Will of God, and He prays that the Will of God be done here on the earth just as it is in heaven. People in heaven are not sick, so we can clearly see it is God's Will that we also be free from sickness and disease.

Deuteronomy 11:21 (NKJV), (If a believer honors God and lives according to the Word, He says...); "That your days and the days of your children may be multiplied in the land which the LORD swore to your fathers to give them, like the days of heaven upon the earth." NOTE–God's plan is for His children to begin to experience the inheritance of the heavenly life while here on the earth. We're already His children, and we have been given special rights. Learning to walk in the Word of God brings the benefits of the Word of God into a living, functioning reality.

Deuteronomy 7:15 (NKJV); "And the LORD will take away from you all sickness, and will afflict you with none of the terrible diseases of Egypt which you have known, but will lay *them* on all those who hate you."

If this was a promise to God's covenant people under the Old Covenant, how much more does this benefit of health pertain to us today; as we are under the New Covenant which is based upon the precious Blood of Jesus Christ?

Romans 8:32 (KJV); "He that spared not his own Son, but delivered him up for us all, how shall he not with him also freely give us all things?" This includes healing!

Mark 16:17-18 (KJV); '[17-]And these signs shall follow them that believe; In my name.... [18-]...they shall lay hands on the sick, and they shall recover."

Find someone who believes God's Word regarding healing, have them lay hands on you and pray for you in faith believing. James 5:16 (KJV) says, "...The effectual fervent prayer of a righteous man avails *[benefits]* much."

Isaiah 40:31 "But they that wait upon the Lord shall renew their strength; they shall mount up with wings as eagles; they shall run, and not be weary, and they shall walk and not faint."

The word "wait" in this verse implies a positive action of hope, based on knowing that the Word of God is a true fact, and it will soon come to pass–waiting with earnest expectation!

Psalm 34:19 (NKJV); "Many *are* the afflictions of the righteous, But the LORD delivers him out of them all."

We often wish we could escape troubles–the pain of grief, loss, sorrow, and failure; or even the small daily frustrations that constantly wear us down. God promises to be "close to the brokenhearted," to be our source of power, courage, and wisdom, helping us through our problems. Sometimes, He chooses to deliver us from those problems. When trouble strikes, don't get frustrated with God. Instead, admit you need His help and thank Him for being by your side.

'Notes'

⇦⇦⇦   Blank page added for 'Notes.'

Blank page added for 'Notes.'

CHAPTER 22

JESUS FINISHED WORK ON THE CROSS

Jesus said, "…When I am lifted up from the earth, I will draw all people to myself."—John 12:32 (NIV).

Jesus took all punishment for our sin. We received the blessing that He deserved.

Hebrews 10:12-14 (KJV); "[12]But this man *[Jesus]*, after he had offered one sacrifice for sins for ever, sat down on the right hand of God; [13] From henceforth expecting till his enemies be made his footstool. [14] For by one offering he hath perfected for ever them that are sanctified."

We have been made perfect, yet we are to continue being made holy. Through His death and resurrection, Christ, once and for all, made His believers perfect in God's sight. At the same time, He is making them holy (progressively cleansed and set apart for His special use) in their daily walk with God here on the earth. We should not be surprised, ashamed, or shocked that we still need to grow spiritually. God is not finished with us. We can encourage this growth process by deliberately applying Scripture to all areas of our lives, by accepting the discipline and guidance Christ

provides, and by giving Him control of our desires and goals.

Romans 5:19 (KJV); "For as by one man's disobedience many were made sinners, so by the obedience of one shall many have been made righteous?"

What a promise this is to those who love Christ! We can reign over sin's power, over death's threats, and over Satan's attacks. Eternal life is ours now and forever. In the power and protection of Jesus Christ, we can overcome temptation. "For he hath made him to be sin for us, who knew no sin; that we might be made the righteousness of God in him."—2 Corinthians 5:21 (KJV).

When we trust in Christ, we make an exchange—our sin for his righteousness. Our sin was poured into Christ at his crucifixion. His righteousness is poured into us at our conversion.

What made Jesus' humanity unique was His freedom from sin. In his full humanity, we can see everything about God's character that can be conveyed in human term.

In Isaiah 53:1-7 & 10-12 (KJV)
1. "Who has believed our report? and to whom is the arm of the Lord revealed?"

This chapter continues to speak of the Messiah, Jesus, who would suffer for the sins of all people. Such a

prophecy is astounding! Who would believe that God would choose to save the world through a humble, suffering servant rather than a glorious king? The idea is contrary to human pride and worldly ways. But God often works in ways we don't expect. Our Messiah's strength is shown by humility, suffering, and mercy.

2. "For he shall grow up before him as a tender plant, and as a root out of a dry ground: he hath no form nor comeliness; and when we shall see him, there is no beauty that we should desire him."

There was nothing beautiful or majestic in the physical appearance of this Jesus. Israel would miscalculate this servant's importance–they would consider Him an ordinary man. But even though Jesus would not attract a large following based on his physical appearance, He would bring salvation and healing for all. Many people miscalculate the importance of Jesus' life and work, and we need faithful Christians to point out his extraordinary nature.

3. "He is despised and rejected of men; a man of sorrows, and acquainted with grief: and we hid as it were our faces from him; he was despised, and we esteemed him not."

This man of sorrows was despised and rejected by those around Him, and He is still despised and rejected by many today. Some reject Christ by standing against Him. Others despise Christ and His great gift of

forgiveness. Do you despise Him, reject Him, or accept Him?

4. "Surely he hath borne our griefs, and carried our sorrows: yet we did esteem him stricken, smitten of God, and afflicted.
5. But he was wounded for our transgressions, he was bruised for our iniquities: the chastisement of our peace was upon him; and with his stripes we are healed.
6. All we like sheep have gone astray; we have turned every one to his own way; and the Lord hath laid on him the iniquity of us all."

Isaiah speaks of Israel straying from God and compares them to wandering sheep. Yet God would send the Messiah (Jesus) to bring them back into the fold. We have the hindsight to see and know the identity of the promised Messiah who has come and died for our sins.

7. "He was oppressed, and he was afflicted, yet he opened not his mouth: he is brought as a lamb to the slaughter, and as a sheep before her shearers is dumb, so he openeth not his mouth."

Isaiah 53:10-12 (KJV)
10. "Yet it pleased the Lord to bruise him; he hath put him to grief: when thou shalt make his soul an offering for sin, he shall see his seed, he shall prolong his days, and the pleasure of the Lord shall prosper in his hand.

11. He shall see of the travail of his soul, and shall be satisfied: by his knowledge shall my righteous servant *[Jesus]* justify many; for he shall bear their iniquities."

'My righteous servant *[Jesus]* justify many,' tells of the enormous family of believers who will become righteous, not by their own works, but by the Messiah's great work on the cross. They are justified because they have claimed Jesus Christ, the righteous servant, as their Savior and Lord (see Romans 10:9, 2 Corinthians 5:21). Their life of sin is stripped away, and they are clothed with Christ's goodness (Ephesians 4:22-24).

12. "Therefore will I divide him a portion with the great, and he shall divide the spoil with the strong; because he hath poured out his soul unto death: and he was numbered with the transgressors; and he bare the sin of many, and made intercession for the transgressors."

In the Old Testament, people offered animals as sacrifices for their sins. Here, the sinless servant of the Lord offers Himself for our sins. He is the Lamb (Isaiah 53:7) offered for the sins of all people (John 1:29; Revelation 5:6-14). The Messiah suffered for our sakes, bearing our sins to make us acceptable to God. What can we say to such love? How will we respond to Him?

John 1:29 (KJV); "The next day John seeth Jesus coming unto him, and saith, Behold the Lamb of God, which taketh away the sin of the world."

Jesus was cursed that we might be blessed.

He paid sin's debt that we might become righteous.

He was despised, that we might be loved.

He was rejected, that we might be favored.

Jesus carried our sorrows that we might be happy.

God smote Him so that God could love us.

He was chastised for our peace.

He bore our iniquities so that we might be free.

All these things Jesus suffered because of his great love for us.

'Notes'

⇦ ⇦ ⇦   Blank page added for 'Notes.'

Blank page added for 'Notes.'

CHAPTER 23

A GLIMPSE OF JESUS IN HEAVEN

Revelation 5:6 (KJV); "And I beheld, and, lo, in the midst of the throne and of the four beasts, and in the midst of the elders, stood a Lamb as it had been slain, having seven horns and seven eyes, which are the seven Spirits of God sent forth into all the earth."

The Lion, Jesus, proved Himself worthy to break the seals and open the scroll by living a perfect life of obedience to God, dying on the cross for the sins of the world, and rising from the dead to show His power and authority over evil and death. Only Christ conquered sin, death, hell, and Satan himself; so only He can be trusted with the world's future.

Jesus Christ is pictured as both a Lion (symbolizing His authority and power) and a Lamb (symbolizing His submission to God's Will). One of the elders calls John to look at the Lion, but when John looks, he sees a Lamb. Christ the Lamb was the perfect sacrifice for the sins of all mankind; therefore, only He can save us from the terrible events revealed by the scroll.

Christ the Lamb won the greatest battle of all. He defeated all the forces of evil by dying on the cross. The role of Christ the Lion will be to lead in the battle

where Satan is finally defeated (Revelation 19:19-21). Christ the Lion is victorious because of what Christ the Lamb has already done. We will participate in this victory, not because of our effort or goodness, but because He has promised eternal life to all who believe in Him.

John sees the Lamb "looking as if it had been slain;" the wounds inflicted on Jesus' body during His trial and crucifixion could still be seen (see John 20:24-31). Jesus was called the Lamb of God by John the Baptist (John 1:29). In the Old Testament, lambs were sacrificed to atone for sins: the Lamb of God died as the final sacrifice for all sins (see Isaiah 53:7; Hebrews 10:1-12 & 18).

Although Christ is a sacrificial lamb, He is in no way weak. He was killed, but now He lives in God's strength and power.

Revelation 5:7-10 (KJV); "[7]And he came and took the book out of the right hand of him that sat upon the throne. [8]And when he had taken the book, the four beasts and four and twenty elders fell down before the Lamb, having every one of them harps, and golden vials full of odors, which are the prayers of saints. [9]And they sung a new song, saying, Thou art worthy to take the book, and to open the seals thereof: for thou wast slain, and hast redeemed us to God by thy blood out of every kindred, and tongue, and people, and nation; [10]And hast made us unto our God kings and priests: and we shall reign on the earth."

People from every nation are praising God before His throne. God's message of salvation and eternal life is not limited to a specific culture, race, or country. Anyone who comes to God in repentance and faith is accepted by Him and will be part of His Kingdom. Don't allow prejudice or bias to keep you from sharing Christ with others. Christ welcomes all people into His Kingdom.

The songs this group is singing praises of Christ's work.

1. He was slain,
2. He purchased us with His blood,
3. Gathered us into His kingdom,
4. Made them priests, and
5. Appointed us to reign on the earth.

Jesus has already died and paid the penalty for sin. He is now gathering us into His Kingdom and making us priests. In the future, we will reign with Him. Worship God and praise Him for what He has done, what He is doing, and what He will do for all who trust in Him. When we realize the glorious future that awaits us, we will find the strength to face our present difficulties.

The believer's song praises Christ for bringing us into His Kingdom and making us kings and priests. While now we are sometimes despised and mocked for our faith (John 15:17-27), in the future we will reign over all the earth (Luke 22:29-30). Christ's death made all

believers priests of God—the channels of blessing between God and mankind (1 Peter 2:5-9).

Revelation 5:11-14 (KJV); "[11-]And I beheld, and I heard the voice of many angels round about the throne and the beasts and the elders: and the number of them was ten thousand times ten thousand, and thousands of thousands; [12-]Saying with a loud voice, Worthy is the Lamb that was slain to receive power, and riches, and wisdom, and strength, and honour, and glory, and blessing. [13-]And every creature which is in heaven, and on the earth, and under the earth, and such as are in the sea, and all that are in them, heard I saying, Blessing, and honour, and glory, and power, be unto him that sitteth upon the throne, and unto the Lamb for ever and ever."

Angels are spiritual beings created by God who help carry out His work on earth. They bring messages (Luke 1:26-28), protect God's people (Daniel 6:22), offer encouragement (Genesis 16:7), give guidance (Exodus 14:19), bring punishment (2 Samuel 24:16), patrol the earth (Ezekiel 1:9-14), and fight the forces of evil (2 Kings 6:16-18, Revelation 20:1).

14. "And the four beasts said, Amen. And the four and twenty elders fell down and worshipped him that liveth for ever and ever."

The scene in Revelation 5 shows us that only the Lamb, Jesus Christ, is worthy to open the scroll (the events that are about to happen). Jesus, not Satan, holds

the future. Jesus Christ is in control, and He alone is worthy to set into motion the events of the last days of history.

God anointed Jesus of Nazareth with the Holy Ghost and with power: who went about doing good and healing all that were oppressed of the devil; for God was with Him.

And when He had called unto Him His twelve disciples, He gave them power against unclean spirits, to cast them out, and to heal all manner of sickness and all manner of disease.

Rise And Be Healed In Jesus Name!

END

'Notes'

⇦⇦⇦   Blank page added for 'Notes.'

Blank page added for 'Notes.'

STUDIES BY DR. ELDON BOLLINGER

Great Commission Bible College
www.gcbcedu.us

1. THE BELIEVER'S NEW LIFE – BENE463–3 HRS.
2. THE DEEPER WALK 1 – DEWA516–4 HRS.
3. THE DEEPER WALK 2 – DEWA517–4 HRS.
4. END TIME EVENTS – ENTI458–8 HRS.
5. FAITH FOR TODAY 1 – FAFO111–3 HRS.
6. FAITH FOR TODAY 2 – FAFO112–5 HRS.
7. SUCCESS THRU THE SCRIPTURE – SUTH553–3 HRS.
8. TEACH ME TO PRAY – TEME512–4 HRS.
9. YOUR BEST IS YET TO COME 1 – YOBE312–3 HRS.
10. YOUR BEST IS YET TO COME 2 – YOBE313–3 HRS.
11. SANCTIFICATION-RIGHTEOUSNESS-HOLINESS 1 – SARI412–3 HRS.
12. SANCTIFICATION-RIGHTEOUSNESS-HOLINESS 2 – SARI413–3 HRS.
13. OUR FINAL GENERATION – OUFI365–3 HRS.
14. JESUS 1 – JESU125–3 HRS.
15. JESUS 2 – JESU126–3 HRS.
16. ISRAEL'S FALL AND REDEMPTION – ISFA145–4 HRS.
17. REVELATION REVEALED 1 – RERE155–3 HRS.
18. REVELATION REVEALED 2 – RERE156–3 HRS.
19. THE AUTHORITY OF THE CHURCH – THAU257–3 HRS.
20. GOD'S PROTECTION PLAN FOR YOU.
21. WHAT ABOUT YOUR FUTURE? – E BOOK.
22. YOUR FUTURE GOD'S WAY – SERIES 1–3 HRS.
23. YOUR FUTURE GOD'S WAY – SERIES 2–3 HRS.
24. YOUR FUTURE GOD'S WAY – SERIES 3–3 HRS.
25. OUR FINAL GENERATION – OUFI365–3 HRS.

My Anointing and Spirit are on all of the above studies and will follow them wherever they go.

Eldon Bollinger

OTHER BOOKS BY DR. ELDON & WANELL BOLLINGER

1. ANGELS
2. CHARACTER – PROVERBS
3. FAITH FOR TODAY
4. FAITH, HOPE, & LOVE – PROVERBS
5. HAPPINESS, KINDNESS, & JOY – PROVERBS
6. JESUS
7. LOVE
8. MISCELLANEOUS – PROVERBS
9. OUR FINAL GENERATION
10. PRAYER THAT MOVES MOUNTAINS
11. PROPHECY & END TIME EVENTS – BOOK 1
12. PROPHECY & END TIME EVENTS – BOOK 2
13. **RISE AND BE HEALED** – (THIS BOOK)
14. SATAN'S TOTAL DEFEAT
15. SUCCESS THROUGH GOD'S WORD
16. TEACH ME TO PRAY
17. THE BELIEVER'S NEW LIFE
18. THE DEEPER WALK – BOOK 1
19. THE DEEPER WALK – BOOK 2
20. WHAT ABOUT YOUR FUTURE
21. WHAT IF I MISS THE RAPTURE
22. WITHOUT HOLINESS, NO MAN SHALL SEE GOD
23. WORDS, WISDOM, & SUCCESS – PROVERBS
24. YOUR BEST IS YET TO COME

VISIT ELDON'S WEBSITE, WWW.ELDONBOLLINGER.COM, AND WWW.AMAZON.COM FOR OTHER BOOKS BY DR. ELDON AND WANELL BOLLINGER.

REFERENCES

BIBLES

(New) American Standard Version	(ASV)-(NASV)
English Standard Version	(ESV)
Living Bible	(LB)
(New) King James Version	(KJV)-(NKJV)-(KJ21)
New International Version	(NIV)
New Living Translation	(NLT)
Weymouth New Testament	(WNT)
Young's Literal Translation	(YLT)

CONTACT US

Dr. Eldon Bollinger's Website: www.eldonbollinger.com

Like Eldon on Facebook:
http://www.facebook.com/eldon.bollinger

Eldon's email address: eldonbollinger@gmail.com

Book Editor—Bob Miller: bob.miller@email.com

ACKNOWLEDGEMENTS

Dr. Harold Bollinger   Chapters 3 and 17

MY COMMISSION

God answered and said, "My son, just as I was with Jesus, so will I be with you. You go and cast out devils. You heal the sick. You cleanse the lepers. You raise the dead. I give you power over all the power of the enemy. Do not be afraid. Be strong. Be courageous. I am with you as I was with Jesus. No demon should be able to stand before you all the days of your life. I used men and women then, but now I desire to use you."

–January 7, 2012

This day will I begin to magnify you in the eyes of the people.

–February 4, 2012

[17] "O God, thou hast taught me from my youth: and hitherto have I declared thy wondrous works.
[18] Now also when I am old and gray-headed, O God, forsake me not; until I have showed thy strength unto *this* generation, *and* thy power to everyone *that* is to come."

–Psalm 71:17–18 (KJV)

Your greatest days are yet ahead, my son.

–January 13, 2013

Eldon Bollinger

~ 191 ~

Blank page added for 'Notes.'

⇦⇦⇦ Blank page added for 'Notes.' ⇨⇨⇨

90401862R00109

Made in the USA
Columbia, SC
02 March 2018